Praying THE SCRIPTURES FOR YOUR Children

Discover How to Pray God's Will for Their Lives

Jodie Berndt

ZondervanPublishingHouse
Grand Rapids, Michigan

A Division of HarperCollins*Publishers*

Praying the Scriptures for Your Children
Copyright © 2001 by Jodie Berndt

Requests for information should be addressed to:
ZondervanPublishingHouse
Grand Rapids, Michigan 49530

Library of Congress Cataloging-in-Publication Data
Berndt, Jodie.
 Praying the scriptures for your children : discover how to pray God's will
for their lives / Jodie Berndt.
   p.   cm.
 Includes bibliographical references.
 ISBN 0-310-23216-3
 1. Mothers—Prayer-books and devotions—English.   2. Children—
Religious life.   I. Title.
BV4847 .B45 2001
248.3'2'0852—dc21   00-051294

This edition is printed on acid-free paper.

Interior design by Melissa Elenbaas

Printed in the United States of America

01 02 03 04 05 06 /❖ DC/ 10 9 8 7 6 5 4 3 2 1

To my parents, Claire and Allen Rundle,
whose steadfast love, faithful example, and constant
prayers have pointed me—and countless others—
toward the God who *loves* us enough
and is *powerful* enough
to do immeasurably more than we could
ever ask or imagine.

Table of Contents

~

Foreword — 9

Acknowledgments — 11

Introduction: Getting Started in Prayer — 13

Part One: Praying for Your Child's Faith

1. Praying for Your Child's Salvation — 21
2. Praying for Your Child to Love God's Word — 32
3. Praying for Your Child's Gifts — 42
4. Praying for Your Child to Promote God's Kingdom — 52

Part Two: Praying for Your Child's Character

5. Praying for Wisdom and Discernment — 65
6. Praying for a Servant's Heart — 76
7. Praying for Kindness and Compassion — 86
8. Praying for Self-Control, Diligence, and Self-Discipline — 96

Part Three: Praying for Your Child's Safety

9. Praying for Physical Health and Safety — 109
10. Praying for Spiritual Protection — 120
11. Praying for Your Child's Emotional Well-Being — 131
12. Praying for Kids in Crisis — 141

Part Four: Praying for Your Child's Relationship ...

13. with Friends	155
14. with Siblings	164
15. with Teachers and Coaches	176
16. with You	188

Part Five: Praying for Your Child's Future

17. Praying for Your Child's Purpose in Life	203
18. Praying for Your Child's Marriage	214
19. Praying for Your Child's Management of Time and Money	226
20. Praying for Your Child When He or She Leaves Your Nest	238

Conclusion: The Life-Changing Work of Prayer	249
Appendix: Using Biblical Characters to Pray for Your Children	254
Recommended Reading and Other Resources	260
Notes	263

Foreword

By: FERN NICHOLS, FOUNDER AND PRESIDENT OF
MOMS IN TOUCH INTERNATIONAL

I BELIEVE THE GREATEST INFLUENCE A MOM CAN HAVE IN THE LIFE of her child is through prayer. As she stands in the gap for her beloved child, the Sovereign Lord of heaven and earth hears and answers her prayers. In this book, Jodie Berndt teaches us simple prayer principles that, if applied, will change your prayer life. One of the most powerful principles is *Scripture praying*. When we pray the promises of God for our children, our faith increases because we are praying back the very words of God. I love this book because I love God's Word, and this book is filled with God's Word. Your soul will be revived, restored, and given great hope as you read it.

I am thrilled to see how God has used Moms In Touch in Jodie's life. She states, "The MITI tactic is to use the Bible itself—God's actual words. Because they come straight out of the Bible, they carry the full weight and power of God's word." Faith in the word of God is the most powerful force there is. Those things we see as impossible mountains in the lives of our children can be removed by praying the promises of Scripture—God's Word.

I appreciate Jodie's vulnerability as a mother. She is a real mom with a real family, facing challenges like every other mom. Jodie honestly portrays the struggles and victories of mothers desiring to be godly women, wanting to raise godly children.

Her humor is uplifting, and the stories will touch your heart. You will be encouraged as you hear how God works in the lives of children through the prayers of their mothers.

When we pray in the name of Jesus, believing the promises of God, His power is released at that moment. Psalm 56:9 declares that the day we call for help, the tide of battle turns. We are in a battle for the very lives of our children. What comforting truth to know that when a righteous mom intercedes, using the Word on behalf of her children, God has heard her prayers and Satan's power is dispelled. Satan's attacks can be destroyed by the power of the living Word of God. Yes, the Word is the most powerful weapon we wield for the protection of our children. I loved taking time at the end of each chapter to actually put my children's names in each one of the recommended Scriptures. It was a faith-building time. I also experienced God's peace flooding my soul as I prayed in faith, believing He would answer my prayers.

What an incredible joy it has been for me to read this book of hope. It is a life-changing book, a book you will want to read, meditate on, pray through, and be encouraged by again and again. My prayer for you is that God the Holy Spirit will grant you increased faith as you believe with all your heart the Scripture promises given for your children in this book, and that it will cause you to search the Scriptures for yourself. I also pray that you will experience, as Jodie has, the joy of answered prayer and loving support that comes from praying with other moms in a Moms In Touch group. The battle for our children's lives is waged in prayer. It is never too late to start praying.

"Father, may You use this book for Your honor and for Your glory. In the precious name of Jesus, Amen."

Acknowledgments

LIKE MOST BOOKS, THIS BOOK BEARS THE NAME OF ONE AUTHOR, but getting the material organized, written, and published has been a group effort. I am indebted to many people for their insight, support, and prayers—especially to my Friday morning Moms In Touch prayer group. Thank you, dear friends, for your willingness to pursue the Lord and seek his very best for our children. What a delight it has been to pray with you, working together in prayer and rejoicing in the awesomeness of God's answers!

Thanks, too, to my other "support group": Lucinda, Camille, Scottie, and (when she agrees to get out of bed) Nancy. Our early-morning runs, undertaken when the days were new and the ideas were fresh, helped generate and shape many of the concepts in this book. You'd make a terrific focus group—at least for market researchers who are willing to talk and run at the same time!

I am grateful, too, for the professionalism, expertise, and loving encouragement so faithfully provided by the folks at Zondervan Publishing House. Thank you to Sandy Vander Zicht for sharing valuable insights right from the start, and to Cindy Hays for taking this ball of a book and running with it. The wisdom, organizational talents, and spiritual maturity you have so generously given to this project enabled me to take a few wobbly thoughts about prayerful parenting and give them a firm place to stand.

I also want to say thank you to my parents, Claire and Allen Rundle, for teaching me how to pray . . . to my siblings, Jen, Mary, and David, for serving as my longest-standing prayer partners . . . and to my in-laws, Mary Lou and Billy Berndt, for loving and encouraging me as one of your own.

An even bigger thank-you goes to my husband, Robbie, the only person in the world who might be happier than I am to see this book finished. Thanks for loving me, encouraging me, and persevering with me—and for repeatedly taking the kids to the zoo so I could get some work done. You're an amazing dad and an even better husband.

And the biggest thanks of all goes to our four loving, noisy, challenging, generous, funny, selfish, precious, incredibly beautiful God-given children: Hillary, Annesley, Virginia Jane, and Robbie. Praying for you—and watching God work in your lives—is one of my favorite things about being a mom. Thanks for your patience as I wrote this book. And please don't grow up and get mad at me when you read what I wrote about you; I tried to keep most of the bad stuff out.

And finally, I am grateful to Jesus Christ, who teaches us to pray, who always intercedes with God on our behalf, and whose life-giving sacrifice is what makes it possible for us to prayerfully approach God's throne of grace with confidence (see Luke 11:1–4; Hebrews 7:25; 4:16).

GETTING STARTED IN PRAYER

This is the confidence we have in approaching God:
that if we ask anything according to his will, he hears us.

— 1 John 5:14

THE BROTHERS GRIMM TELL THE STORY OF *SLEEPING BEAUTY*, which opens with all of the fairies in the kingdom bringing baptismal gifts to an infant princess. One fairy gives beauty, another offers virtue, a third bestows kindness, and so on until the little girl has everything she needs to grow into a wise and lovely young woman.

Reading this story to my own young daughters, I used to wish that such blessings were so easy to come by. Just throw a christening party, invite all the fairies, and—presto!—your child would be covered.

But God gives us another—better—way to provide these gifts (and so many more) for our children. He invites us to pray. And, in fact, according to many biblical scholars, God *requires* us to pray before he can go to work. About 250 years ago, British evangelist John Wesley wrote that "God does nothing on earth save in answer to believing prayer"; many contemporary pastors and authors echo this thought, noting, as nineteenth-century evangelist Andrew Murray did, that "God's giving is inseparably connected with our asking."[1]

The Bible supports this connection. Over and over again God says, *"Ask of me, and I will ..."* and *"If my people ... will humble themselves and pray, ... then will I ..."* and *"Ask and it will be given to you."*[2] Moreover, there is scriptural evidence that there are times when our failure to ask God for something results in his holding back on the blessings or protection he wanted to provide (see, for example, Ezekiel 22:30–31). No matter how you interpret passages like this one, one thing is clear: *God wants us to pray.*

As a mother, I've always seen prayer as a natural part of the parenting process, and I have always prayed for my children. But for many years my prayers tended to run along the "God bless Johnny" lines. I'd ask God to help my kids on their spelling tests, protect them on field trips, and restore their health when they got the flu or ran a fever. Rarely, though, did my prayers get more creative than that, and almost never did I sense that they packed any real punch.

And then I got involved with a group called Moms In Touch. On the basis of Scripture verses like John 15:7 ("If you remain in me and my words remain in you, ask whatever you wish, and it will be given you") and Jeremiah 1:12, AMPLIFIED ("I am alert *and* active, watching over My word to perform it"), the Moms In Touch prayer tactic is to use the Bible itself—God's actual words—as the foundation for our prayers.

Here's what I mean. Verses like Ephesians 4:32 ("Be kind and compassionate to one another, forgiving each other, just as in Christ God forgave you") can be reworked into terrific prayers for how your kids treat each other:

I pray that Hillary and Annesley would be kind and compassionate toward each other, forgiving each other just as in Christ God forgave them.

Verses like 2 Timothy 2:22 ("Flee the evil desires of youth, and pursue righteousness, faith, love and peace, along with those who call on the Lord out of a pure heart") can serve as a prayer for the friends your children choose:

I pray that Virginia and Robbie would flee from evil desires and pursue righteousness, faith, love, and peace, enjoying the company of children who call on the Lord and have pure hearts.

Not only are prayers like these more interesting and creative than the ones I used to come up with on my own, but, because they come straight out of the Bible, they carry the full weight and power of God's word. As God says in Isaiah 55:11, "my word ... will not return to me empty, but will accomplish what I desire and achieve the purpose for which I sent it." And as the author of Hebrews points out, "the Word that God speaks is alive and full of power [making it active, operative, energizing, and effective]."[3]

Using the Bible as the basis for many of my prayers made them more interesting, creative, and powerful, but I still found myself hanging back, more comfortable sitting on the bench than actually charging onto the playing field of Serious Prayer. Serious Prayer was, I figured, reserved for life's *real* Prayer Warriors—people who had fewer kids and a lot less laundry to do than I did. Reading about Christians who spent hours in prayer did little to inspire me; in fact, it made me want to give up and throw in the prayer towel. "I'm just not that holy," I'd tell myself. "I'm just not like that."

Then I met Cynthia Heald, a best-selling author whose books include one called *Becoming a Woman of Prayer*. "I'd like to be a 'woman of prayer,'" I told her, "but I'm not. The way I see it, if I don't spend at least a half hour sitting down, with my notebook and Bible in hand, and really *pray*, then my prayers won't count."

Cynthia set me straight. "You can pray in the car pool line," she said, "or while you're washing dishes. Pray while you walk through your neighborhood, or while you clean the bathroom. It doesn't take a lot of time or preparation to meet God. Just go to him, and you're there."

Now, I am sure that Cynthia Heald would encourage all of us to make time in our daily schedules for some concentrated, uninterrupted prayer, but her gentle advice to "just do it" got me started. I began to pray while I drove, while I made lunches, while I cleaned—and I even added my own little trick. Thinking of the temple incense that wafted toward heaven in Bible times, I began to use the smell of Lysol or Tilex as my own "fragrant" reminder to send my prayers heavenward while I scrubbed the toilet!

No matter how limited your own prayer life might be, it can't be as pathetic as that.

I love my kids—Hillary, Annesley, Virginia Jane, and Robbie. And I know you love your kids. Don't let Satan rob you of the joy of praying for them—and of seeing God work in their lives—by making you think you're somehow not up to the job.

Each of the chapters in this book deals with a different prayer topic or area of concern that parents often have for their children. Each chapter includes illustrations that bring these topics to life, and while I have sometimes changed names and minor details, all of the stories are true. I am grateful to the many parents who were willing to share in this book their concerns as well as their prayers.

At the end of each chapter I've included several Bible verses written in the form of prayers you can personalize for your family. You can use just one of these prayer verses, or pray your way through all of them. You can read and pray through all twenty chapters, or pick and choose the sections that appeal to you. Once you find out what's here, you might want to use this book as a reference manual of sorts for those times when your kids come to a tough spot and you need some fresh ideas for prayer.

Pastor and author Jack Hayford likens prayer to a "partnership of the redeemed child of God working hand in hand with God toward the realization of his redemptive purposes on earth."[4] As you slip your hand into your heavenly Father's, prayerfully working with him to see his purposes fulfilled in the lives of your children, my prayer is that you will come face-to-face with the God of Ephesians 3:20—the One who is able to do immeasurably more than all you could ask or imagine.

Sleeping Beauty may have had a bevy of fairies in her nursery, but we have access to the throne room of the King of kings. And given a choice between the two, I know which one I'd pick.

What about you?

Part One

Praying for Your Child's Faith

CHAPTER ONE

PRAYING FOR YOUR CHILD'S SALVATION

Jesus said, "Let the little children come to me,
and do not hinder them, for the kingdom of
heaven belongs to such as these."

—Matthew 19:14

JULIE GREW UP IN A HOME WHERE CHURCH ATTENDANCE WAS SPO-
radic and Jesus was never mentioned by name. It wasn't until
high school that she found out who Christ really was. She
became a Christian then, and, years later, when she married her
high school sweetheart, she resolved that things would be different when they had their own family. They would introduce
their kids to Jesus at an early age and bring them up to love and
fear God. Secretly, though, Julie wondered whether she could do
it. The Christian life had never been modeled for her as a child;
how was she supposed to teach her children everything she had
missed? What if she blew it? What if they didn't respond? What
if they rejected the faith she held so dear?

Mollie had no such doubts. She and her husband strode confidently into parenthood, armed with principles gleaned from countless seminars, books, and personal devotions. They "cleansed" their home of anything that might be an obstacle to faith: out went secular books, movies, and music; in came Bible stories, family-oriented games and sports, and praise songs. Theirs was a close-knit, "model" Christian family in every way—until their oldest son met and fell in love with a Muslim girl in college. *Where,* Mollie wondered, *had they gone wrong? Had they pushed their kids too hard? Would her son abandon his Christian convictions for this girl?*

Barbara didn't become a Christian until four years after her divorce, at a time when her children were well into their teenage years. She had no illusions about her limitations; as a single mom it was all she could do to make ends meet, let alone offer her kids much in the way of emotional support or guidance. She assumed, as most of her friends did, that her kids would naturally experiment with things like sex, drugs, and alcohol—she just hoped that nobody would get pregnant. But when Barbara met Christ, she began to wonder, *Was there hope for her kids? Or had the divorce, their financial struggles, and the total lack of any sort of Christian influence or instruction left them "too far gone" for God?*

Julie, Mollie, and Barbara are not their real names, but these women are all friends of mine. Their questions are genuine. The good news for them (and for all of us) is that God is not bound by our human failings. No matter how many parenting mistakes we make, his grace is more than sufficient to cover them. The bad news is that no matter how many things we do right in terms of pointing our kids toward Christ, we cannot *make* them love the Lord. We cannot force them into faith or convince them that God's grace is real. As Jesus put it in John 6:44, "No one can come to me unless the Father who sent me draws him."

Does the fact that only God can draw people to himself mean that our job as mothers (or fathers) is simply to sit around and watch? Absolutely not. *Experiencing God* author Henry Blackaby says that seeing God at work is our invitation to adjust our lives and join him.[1] As parents, we can "join God" in countless ways: We can expose our children to stories of God's faithfulness and protection; we can model the Christian life and introduce them to other believers; we can teach them, encourage them, sing to them, and love them. And most of all, we can pray for them.

The sooner we realize that it is not about what *we* do but about what *God* does, the sooner we will stop focusing on ourselves and our shortcomings, and begin focusing on God and his power. Likewise, the sooner we quit worrying about doing our part, the sooner we can start rejoicing in the fact that God is doing his part. And the sooner we recognize that God *is* at work, the sooner we can jump in and join him.

Prayer Principle _____

When you pray for your children, you join
God in the work he is doing in their lives.

_____ ✑

Salvation as the Starting Point

Before I started writing this book, I polled more than one hundred mothers to see what they wanted most for their children. My informal surveys, tucked into our family's Christmas cards and randomly distributed to friends and neighbors, listed everything from health and safety to academic success and strong family ties. I asked folks to check their top five desires or prayer requests, and I eventually used this feedback to shape the book's table of contents.

On the survey I also included an "other" category, where folks could comment on the topics or add their own thoughts. My friend Troy Lee shared this story of how God answered her prayers for her children:

> Before each of my children was born I prayed that they would be *first* a Christian and *second* healthy. I prayed that as long as we would be allowed to enjoy our children on earth, it would be long enough for them to accept Christ as their Savior. In other words, please let them live to be saved—however old or however young.
>
> This prayer has been answered for two of my children so far, but very significantly in Abner IV's life. You may know that he died at age seven and a half. Seven months prior to his unexpected death, Abner prayed with his father to accept Christ and was baptized the next week. God let him live long enough to be saved.
>
> This is even more interesting as we found out exactly what Abner died of (it took nine weeks to determine). Endocardial fibroelastosis is very rare. We were told that Abner's case would be published in a medical journal because in the last forty years, only two other people in the world had ever lived past age one with this condition.

And I keep thinking, *God let him live long enough to be saved*. Praise Him!

Isn't this an amazing story? Where others might see only pain and loss, Troy Lee recognized the hand of God and the answer to her prayers. But, you might ask, shouldn't she have asked God to make her children healthy—*no matter what*? And if she had, would she have been spared the anguish of losing a child?

I can't answer these questions, but I know that in placing her children's salvation at the top of her prayer list—and in praying for them even before they were born—Troy Lee demonstrated an incredible maturity and depth of insight. She recognized what so many of us miss: that a relationship with the Savior is more important than anything else. A child can be blessed with a healthy body, good grades, an outstanding character, a wealth of friends, and an athletic scholarship to the college of his or her choice—but without a relationship with Jesus, it all counts for nothing.

Prayer Principle _____

Praying for your children's salvation is asking God to give them the only gift that lasts forever.

Never Give Up

Salvation may be the starting point of our prayers for our children, but God doesn't always answer this prayer first.

Praying for our children to know and love God often demands incredible patience, perseverance, and trust.

Helen has been praying for her three children for more than twenty years. Two of them love the Lord; one is what Helen calls "a work in progress." As she looks at the young mothers in her church, Helen remembers the days when nurturing her children's faith came easily, as their little hearts opened up to the Bible stories she read, the songs she sang, and the prayers she prayed. Now, though, Helen knows what it means to weep for her children, to long for them to come to faith, and to cry out to God on their behalf. "We mothers who have older children really grieve when they are not in the fold," she says.

Even so, Helen is not discouraged. Holding on to verses like Habakkuk 2:3 ("Though [the revelation] linger, wait for it; it will certainly come and will not delay"), she envisions the day when all three of her children will have a vibrant relationship with the Lord, and she is quick to encourage other mothers with some of the promises God has given her:

- " 'Restrain your voice from weeping and your eyes from tears, for your work will be rewarded,' declares the LORD. 'They will return from the land of the enemy. So there is hope for your future. . . . Your children will return to their own land.' "—Jeremiah 31:16–17
- "All your sons will be taught by the LORD, and great will be your children's peace."—Isaiah 54:13
- "I will repay you for the years the locusts have eaten . . . and you will praise the name of the LORD your God, who has worked wonders for you."—Joel 2:25–26

Along with promises like these, Helen has the assurance that her prayers line up perfectly with God's will for her children's lives. As 2 Peter 3:9 says, "The Lord is not slow in keeping his promise, as some understand slowness. He is patient with you, not wanting anyone to perish, but everyone to come to repentance." God wants our children to be saved.

Prayer Principle _____

When you pray for your children's salvation, you can be confident that you are praying in accordance with God's will.

_____ ∾

Poised for Prayer

If you are like Helen, and you have prayed long and hard for your children's salvation, you may be wondering why God has not yet answered your prayers. Author Jeanne Hendricks points to the example of Elizabeth, who lived faithfully and righteously despite the heartache of her inability to have children. But rather than become bitter over this unanswered prayer, Elizabeth chose to trust God and wait on him. As a result, she acquired an inner strength and fortitude that, Hendricks says, allowed her to become a "stronger woman and a better mother."[2] Eventually, Elizabeth gave birth to John the Baptist—and God used her to encourage and strengthen Mary, the mother of Jesus.[3]

"Godly patience," Hendricks says, "is the art of letting God set the timer." Whether you are just beginning to pray for your children, or whether you have spent years holding them up before the Lord, here are three things you can do to develop godly patience and the same kind of inner strength that sustained Elizabeth:

First, pray with an attitude of thanksgiving. Colossians 4:2 says, "Devote yourselves to prayer, being watchful and thankful." Remember that God loves your children, and that he does not want them to perish. Thank him for the work he is doing in their lives—even if you cannot see it at the moment.

Next, build your faith. Memorize verses like 1 John 5:14–15: "This is the confidence we have in approaching God: that if we ask anything according to his will, he hears us. And if we know that he hears us—whatever we ask—we know that we have what we asked of him." Ask God to show you promises from his Word and make them a focal point of your prayer life. You can use the verses at the end of this chapter if you like, and insert your child's name into the blanks to turn them into personal prayers.

Finally, be persistent. In Luke 18:1, Jesus tells us that we should "always pray and not give up." Whether we are praying for our children's salvation or for something else, we can benefit from this advice found in the book of Hebrews: "You need to persevere so that when you have done the will of God, you will receive what he has promised."[4]

～ Prayers You Can Use ～

Heavenly Father...

Remove the veil from _____'s eyes so that he can see the light of the gospel. Shine your light in his heart to give him

the light of the knowledge of your glory in the face of
Christ. (2 Corinthians 4:4–6)

∾

*P*ut people in _____'s life who will gently instruct her; and
grant her repentance leading to a knowledge of the truth.
Cause _____ to come to her senses and escape from the
trap of the devil, who has taken her captive to do his will.
(2 Timothy 2:25–26)

∾

*O*pen _____'s eyes and turn him from darkness to light,
and from the power of Satan to God, so that he may receive
forgiveness of sins and a place among those who are sanc-
tified by faith in Christ. (Acts 26:18)

∾

*D*on't let _____ be haunted by her past. Remind her that
if anyone is in Christ, she is a new creation; the old has
gone, the new has come! (2 Corinthians 5:17)

∾

I pray that _____ would confess with his mouth that Jesus
is Lord, and that he would believe in his heart that you have
raised Christ from the dead. Cause _____ to call on your
name, Lord, and save him. (Romans 10:9, 13)

∾

Thank you for loving _____ *so much that you gave your one and only Son, that when* _____ *believes in him she will not perish but have eternal life. (John 3:16)*

∾

I pray that _____ *would continue to live in Christ, rooted and built up in him, strengthened in the faith as he was taught, and overflowing with thankfulness. (Colossians 2:6–7)*

∾

Count _____ *as one of your people, and be her God. Give her a singleness of heart and action, so that she will always fear you for her own good and for the good of her children. Make an everlasting covenant with* _____. *Never stop doing good to her, and inspire her to fear you so that she will never turn away from you. (Jeremiah 32:39–40)*

∾

Put a new spirit in _____. *Remove his heart of stone and give him a heart of flesh. Cause* _____ *to follow your decrees and keep your laws. Let him know that he belongs to you, and that you are his God. (Ezekiel 11:19)*

∾

I pray that _____ *would put her trust in you and never be shaken. (Psalm 125:1)*

∾

I pray that _____, being rooted and established in love, may have power, together with all the saints, to grasp how wide and long and high and deep is the love of Christ, and to know this love that surpasses all understanding, that _____ may be filled to the measure of all the fullness of God. (Ephesians 3:18–19)

CHAPTER TWO

PRAYING FOR YOUR CHILD TO LOVE GOD'S WORD

I have hidden your word in my heart
that I might not sin against you.

—Psalm 119:11

I LOOKED UP FROM MY GARDENING TO SEE MY TWO YOUNGEST CHIL-dren, Virginia and Robbie, in animated conversation. They made such a pretty picture, sitting in the grass with the sunlight dappling their little blond heads, that I couldn't resist creeping closer to listen. Picking up my trowel and a clay pot, I inched forward and made a pretense of planting a few geraniums.

As I fiddled with the flowers, five-year-old Virginia plucked a handful of long green acuba leaves from a nearby bush and handed several to her three-year-old brother. "Now wave them," she commanded.

Robbie complied, and Virginia continued to talk. " ... they saw him coming on his donkey," she said, "and they waved their branches, saying 'Hosanna! Hosanna! Blessed is he who comes in the name of the Lord!'"

Watching the two of them wave their leaves to dramatize the story of Jesus' last days on earth, I wanted to laugh out loud—more from delight than from amusement. Virginia told the story with such passion ("They put *nails* into his *hands*, Robbie! *NAILS!*") that I found myself drawn into their little circle, overwhelmed by the power in her simple words. Speaking in the language of a five-year-old, she managed to communicate the anguish of the cross, the fear and confusion of Christ's followers, and the incredible triumph of the resurrection—all in the space of about two minutes.

"Now," Virginia concluded suddenly, breaking the spell, "*you* tell the story, Robbie. Start with the part where the disciples found the donkey."

God's Word: Guiding Light, Protective Shield

As this story illustrates, a love of Scripture can begin at an early age. How well we "read-aloud" moms know the tender joy of snuggling a small one on our lap or tucking him into bed with an adventure-come-to-life from the pages of a colorfully illustrated children's Bible.

But these bedtime rituals are only the beginning. Psalm 119:105 likens God's word—his laws, his commandments, his promises—to a lamp that sheds light on our path. Perhaps nowhere is this guiding light more necessary (or more welcome!) than when our children have outgrown our laps, when peer relationships, academic challenges, and other pressure points can generate a cloud of darkness or confusion in their lives.

Our prayers are undoubtedly the first line of defense against these clouds—and against the satanic schemes and assaults they often mask. Make no mistake: Satan wants to destroy our families, and he is always on the lookout for ways to sow seeds of tension, rebellion, and destruction. As 1 Peter 5:8 warns, "Your enemy the devil prowls around like a roaring lion looking for someone to devour." But important as it is for us to pray, it is equally vital for our kids to be equipped to withstand Satan's attacks when they come. And their number one defense against the devil's pressures and temptations is the knowledge and prayerful application of Scripture.

Prayer Principle _____

> Praying for your children to know, love, and use God's word is one of the most effective ways to pray for their spiritual protection.

Learning from Jesus' Example

Here's an example of how this defense can work. In Luke 4, the devil finds Jesus in the desert, hungry and alone. "Tell this stone to become bread," Satan suggests. Jesus replies, "It is written: 'Man does not live on bread alone.'"

Next, Satan shows Jesus all the kingdoms of the world. "If you worship me," he says, "it will all be yours." Here again, Jesus doesn't argue; instead, he simply says, "It is written: 'Worship the Lord your God and serve him only.'"

Finally, Satan takes Jesus to the top of the temple and says (my paraphrase), "If you are the Son of God, throw yourself down from here. The angels will lift you up in their hands—you won't get hurt!" Once again, Jesus refuses to take the bait, choosing to quote another Scripture verse: "It says: 'Do not put the Lord your God to the test.'"

Jesus withstands the devil's schemes—not through intellectual prowess, physical strength, or willpower, but simply by knowing and using God's word. And like Jesus, the child or teenager who has moved beyond bedtime stories to the place where he knows and loves the Bible will be well-equipped to withstand the attacks and temptations that come his way. The pressures themselves do not disappear; rather, they become easier to address, given the lessons learned from Scripture.

God's commands are not meant to limit our freedom. Rather, they are meant to protect us and show us how to live life to the fullest. Let's pray that our children will see God's word for what it is: a guiding light that illuminates the pathway to God's blessings. Let's pray, according to Psalm 119:11, that our kids will love God's word, hiding it in their hearts to keep them from sinning against God and interfering with the blessings he wants to provide.

Prayer Principle _____

When you ask God to hide his word in your child's heart, you are asking him for the blessings of wisdom, protection, and freedom.

A Teenage Transformation

Our friends, Gail and Tim, have four active, intelligent children. Gail is one of the most energetic mothers I know, and she is always coming up with new ideas for family devotions and Christ-centered celebrations. Some time ago, though, she confided to me that she found it increasingly difficult to deal with the changing needs of all four kids.

Their oldest child, Emily, had just entered high school. Devotional subjects that appealed to the younger children failed to capture her interest, and the pressures of homework, peer relationships, and after-school sports tended to limit the time Emily was willing to spend on things like prayer and Bible study. "I could force her to participate," Gail told me, "but what Tim and I really want—and what we constantly pray for—is to see Emily start taking the initiative on her own."

Several months later, their prayers were answered when Emily volunteered at a summer camp run by Young Life, a national organization that shares the gospel with high school students. There she forged friendships with other teens on the work crew, and, almost without realizing it, Emily found herself imitating the habits of the other volunteers. She began to spend time reading her Bible, and she looked forward to discussing what she had read with her coworkers.

Emily spent a month at the camp, and when she returned, Gail and Tim couldn't help but notice the transformation. Gail was delighted when Emily decided to give her best friend a devotional book so that the two of them could study the Bible together. Emily seemed like a new person, and in the last few weeks of summer, her faith seemed to grow by leaps and bounds.

Then school started again. Classes hadn't even been in session for a week when the "old Emily" began to reappear. She won a spot on the varsity soccer team, and that—coupled with the heavy workload in her college prep curriculum—left her with little time to get together with friends, and even less room in her schedule for Bible reading and study. "She's pretty stressed-out," Gail told me. "Please pray for her."

I did pray for Emily—and as I did, I was reminded of the Parable of the Sower, found in Luke 8:1–15. In this story, a farmer sows his seed. Some of the seed falls on a path, where it gets trampled and eaten by birds. Some lands on rocky ground, and the plants die for lack of water. Other seed falls among thorns, which grow up and choke the plants. And some falls on good soil, yielding a hundredfold crop.

In answer to his disciples' questions, Jesus explains the parable. "The seed is the word of God," he says. Each of the soils—the path, the rocks, the thorns, and the good soil—represent a different heart condition. As I prayed for Emily, a picture of a healthy plant being choked by thorns—homework, sports, peer pressures and relationships, family life, busy schedules—came to mind. I began to pray according to Luke 8:15, that Emily's heart would be "good soil," and that she would "hear the word, retain it, and by persevering produce a crop."

As I write this, Gail and I are still waiting to see how God will answer our prayers. Although we don't know what his answer will look like, we are confident that it *will* come, since God always keeps his promises. One of those promises comes from Matthew 18:19–20: "If two of you on earth agree about anything you ask for, it will be done for you by my Father in heaven. For where two or three come together in my name, there am I with them." I feel privileged to agree with Gail in prayer for her daughter—and I count Gail's prayers for my children as one of the greatest blessings of our friendship.

Prayer Principle _____

Enlisting the support of a praying friend multiplies the power of your prayers and invites God into your prayer circle.

_____ ∾

Poised for Prayer

One of the best ways we can foster a love for God's word is to encourage our kids to memorize Scripture. Young children, especially, have a seemingly limitless capacity for memorization—a lesson I learned when Hillary, as a three-year-old, recited the entire preamble to the *Beauty and the Beast* story on video, word for word. For me, that did it: I figured that any child who could recite a Hollywood script could certainly learn a couple of Bible verses!

I laughed the other day when my friend Susan told me how adept her daughter, Christie Ray, was at Bible memory—so much so that Susan suggested to the third grader that she consider using her skill as her "talent" in the school talent show. Christie Ray—not too surprisingly—balked at the idea, but I got a kick out of it, and I am thrilled by the possibilities of what God can do in the life of a girl who has so diligently hidden his word in her heart. I am excited, too, by the protection

Christie Ray's "talent" offers. I remember hearing about a would-be con man who found that every time he tried to pull a fast one, the Bible verses he learned as a child would spring to mind to keep him honest!

From providing direction to offering protection, the Bible is brimming with promises that pertain to God's word and its usefulness for our lives. In addition to the prayers listed below, you can use a concordance to find other passages on this subject. Start by looking up words like "word" and "commands." You'll find a treasure trove of powerful promises you can shape into prayers for your family.

Prayers You Can Use

Heavenly Father...

Let _____ keep your words and store up your commands so that he will live. Cause him to guard your teachings as the apple of his eye, and let them be written on the tablet of his heart. (Proverbs 7:2–3)

Show _____ that your way is perfect and your word is flawless. Be her shield as she takes refuge in you. (2 Samuel 22:31)

Show _____ *that all Scripture is God-breathed and is useful for teaching, rebuking, correcting, and training in righteousness. (2 Timothy 3:16)*

∽

Let _____'s *heart be good soil, that he might hear your word, retain it, and persevere to produce a crop of godly character and effectiveness for your kingdom. Don't let Satan snatch your word from* _____'s *heart, and don't let the worries, riches, or pleasures of this life choke your word and make it unfruitful in his life. Let his roots go down deep, so he can stand firm in times of testing. (Luke 8:11–15)*

∽

Let _____ *take delight in your law, and let her meditate on it day and night, so that whatever she does will prosper. (Psalm 1:1–3)*

∽

Teach _____ *to know your commands and obey them, thereby demonstrating his love for you. Let him know your promised reward: that "he who loves me will be loved by my Father, and I too will love him and show myself to him." Love him, and show yourself to him, Lord. (John 14:21)*

∽

Do not let _____ merely listen to the word, and so deceive herself. Let her do what it says. (James 1:22)

∾

Let the word of Christ dwell in _____ richly as he and his peers teach and admonish one another with all wisdom, and as he sings psalms, hymns, and spiritual songs with gratitude in his heart toward God. (Colossians 3:16)

∾

May _____ not live on bread alone, but on every word that comes from the mouth of God. (Matthew 4:4)

∾

Make your word a lamp to _____'s feet and a light for her path. (Psalm 119:105)

CHAPTER THREE

PRAYING FOR YOUR CHILD'S GIFTS

Each one should use whatever gift he has
received to serve others, faithfully administering
God's grace in its various forms.

— 1 Peter 4:10

WHEN OUR DAUGHTER ANNESLEY WAS THREE YEARS OLD, SHE LOVED to work on puzzles. She had an unusual system. Rather than fitting the edge pieces together or tackling certain sections of the picture, she would methodically work from left to right, trying each of the two or three hundred tiny pieces in sequence like some sort of towheaded computer. Slowly but surely, the scene would reveal itself, as though an unseen hand were drawing back the curtain.

Later, when she learned to write, Annesley became a list maker. At night, she would pick out clothes to wear to school the next day, and then make a list of the clothes and how they were to be worn ("Pull socks up to knees"), which she placed on top of the pile of clothes, just in case she forgot anything. Last New Year's Eve I found her making a list of ten carefully defined resolutions, all written in capital letters: TALK TO GOD EVERY DAY, EXERCISE EVERY SATURDAY, COMPLETE HOMEWORK BEFORE ANYTHING....

In addition to making lists, Annesley likes to clean out her drawers, label sections of her closet according to season, and keep track of things like homework, appointments, and family vacations on the calendar she got from the orthodontist. For a long time, I regarded this behavior as little more than a funny quirk. After all, none of my other kids were so compulsive, and I didn't know any other seven- or eight-year-olds who begged to make chore charts for the family to follow.

Ashamed as I am to admit it, it wasn't until I started doing the research for this chapter that I realized that Annesley has the *gift* of organization. She is more than just a chart-making list keeper: She makes hard jobs look easy, she pays attention to details, and she can visualize a goal and decide on the steps she needs to take to achieve it. She has a special, God-given talent.

Speaker and author Susan Alexander Yates advises parents to pay attention to the gifts God gives their children, and clue them in on the fact that God has given them these talents or abilities for a purpose. "A sense of destiny will encourage our children," she says. "Learning to recognize their gifts will enable them to discern more clearly the ways in which God might use them."[1]

Two days after reading Susan's advice, I had the opportunity to put it into practice. The kids and I were walking home from school when Annesley blurted out her plans: "When we get home I'm going to pack my bag for the sleepover tomorrow, then get a snack, and then work on my homework, okay, Mom?"

"Annesley," I replied, "I really appreciate how organized you are. God has given you a special gift. Won't it be exciting to see how he uses your talents to bless other people?"

The look on Annesley's face sent a stab through my heart. She was positively *beaming*. Seeing her reaction to my words, I realized that I had rarely—if ever—commented on her talent for organization, and I had never told her how grateful I was that God had gifted her in that way. How could I have been so negligent? I don't know. But there is one thing I am sure of: Never again will I pass up the chance to point out my kids' gifts and encourage them to use them for God's kingdom.

Prayer Principle _____

> Praying for your children to recognize their giftedness can help them gain a sense of destiny as they consider the ways God might use them.

_____

Diamonds in the Rough

James 1:17 says, "Every good and perfect gift is from above." But while the gifts God gives us may be perfect, we don't always use them in the right way. Perfect gifts in the hands of imperfect people can wind up looking more like liabilities than like assets.

For instance, organizers are often good delegators, but they can be bossy. They can see how to get a job done but fail to explain it well enough so others can grasp their vision. They can tend to put projects ahead of people. How do I know? Because I am an organizer—and I pray that in sharing my gifts, Annesley will be spared my tendencies to misuse them.

Knowing that gifts can be misused can help us as parents to stop focusing on our kids' negative traits and start nurturing their underlying talents and abilities. For instance, Hillary was a shy, quiet, and sometimes overly sensitive preschooler. As she has grown in her relationship with the Lord, however, we have seen these traits blossom into gifts of gentleness, compassion, and mercy. At age ten, she is far more apt than the rest of us to reach out to a lonely or hurting child, and she already demonstrates a keen sensitivity to the Holy Spirit.

Likewise, five-year-old Virginia's stubborn, independent streak will one day (we pray!) enable her to resist peer pressure and proclaim the gospel, regardless of what others think of her. And who knows? Maybe three-year-old Robbie's tendency to hoard the pennies and nickels he finds around the house and hide candy under his bed will eventually reveal themselves as precursors to the thriftiness, resourcefulness, and financial discernment that mark those who have the gift of giving!

Next time your fourth grader puts off doing his homework so he can entertain your friend's preschool-aged children when she stops by for a visit, thank God for giving him the gift of service. Next time your teenager berates a younger sibling for leaving the CD player on overnight, consider the fact that she might have the strong sense of right and wrong that often characterizes God's prophets. And when your twelve-year-old fails to come home on time for dinner because he was talking with the recently widowed gentleman who lives up the street, bear in mind that he may have the gift of mercy.

I am not, of course, suggesting that we excuse things like irresponsibility, harsh words, or disobedience. On the contrary, we need to do all we can to correct our kids when they veer off the track or show signs of misusing their talents. But when our kids frustrate or disappoint us (as they surely will), let's ask God to show us how to turn their mistakes or shortcomings into talent-sharpening opportunities. After all, even the most brilliant diamonds start out as dull, grayish lumps.

Prayer Principle _____

> When you ask God to help you identify and appreciate the unique gifts he has given your children, you invite him to show you your kids as he sees them: glimmering diamonds hidden in the rough.

Fitting into God's Plan

Our friends Pelle and Evie have two of the most obviously gifted children we know. Even as a young child, Jenny demonstrated a talent for public speaking and communications, while her older brother, Kris, distinguished himself as an accomplished musician and a technological whiz kid. By the time these kids reached high school, they had done things many adults only dream of—including writing, producing, and performing in television programs designed to reach young children with the gospel.

Pelle believes such accomplishments are no accident. Pointing to the prophet Jeremiah, Pelle says that God knows us before we are born, and that he has a plan for us right from the start. "We think God looks at us and says, 'Oh, boy, look how talented he is. I think I'll use him to do such and such,'" Pelle comments. "But in reality, God gives us gifts and talents long before we are capable of doing anything. He appointed Jeremiah to be a prophet, and Jeremiah was still crying in his crib. Nobody else knew it—but God did."[2]

Pelle and Evie are grateful for the creativity their children demonstrate. Even so, they recognize that it is all too easy for parents (and kids) to become consumed by a child's giftedness. Ephesians 4:12 says that the gifts God gives us are meant to build up the body of Christ, but these gifts can also be used for carnal and worldly purposes. "Our job," Pelle says, "is not so much to develop our kids' gifts and talents as it is to encourage them to stay close to the Lord. We often tell our children that it doesn't matter what they do—simple or great—as long as they walk close to the Lord. *That's* when they will be truly successful, and that's when they will be able to do God's work."

Prayer Principle _____

Praying that your children will stay close to the Lord can help them yield their gifts and talents to accomplish his purposes.

Poised for Prayer

When Jesus appeared to his disciples after his resurrection, he told them to wait for the gift God would send, a gift that would empower them to spread the gospel to the ends of the earth.[3] That gift was the Holy Spirit, and just as God promised to give the Holy Spirit to the disciples, so he promises to give him to us. As Luke 11:13 puts it, "If you then, though you are evil, know how to give good gifts to your children, how much more will your Father in heaven give the Holy Spirit to those who ask him!"

Do you want your kids' lives to be marked by joy? Do you want them to display contentment and gratitude? Do you want them to be encouragers, good listeners, and passionate about leading others to Christ? Would you love to see them exercise their God-given creativity through music, art, or mechanical skill? All these gifts (and countless others) come from God himself, and they are manifested in our lives through the work of the Holy Spirit.

If praying for the Holy Spirit to work in your children's lives is an unfamiliar concept, you might want to read up on how God's Spirit works, the kinds of gifts he offers, and the ways Christians are urged to use these gifts. Start with passages like Acts 2, Galatians 5, and 1 Corinthians 12 and 14, and then if you want to dig deeper, get out a concordance and look up words like *Spirit* and *gifts*.

As parents, we want to give our kids the very best. Likewise, our heavenly Father longs to shower them with blessings and equip them with everything they need to love him deeply and serve him effectively. When you think about the gifts you want to give to your children, think big. Ask God to empower them through the Holy Spirit—and then watch as he blesses them with gifts, talents, and abilities that are far better than anything you could imagine.

❧ Prayers You Can Use ❧

Heavenly Father...

Let _____ use his gift to serve others, faithfully administering your grace in its various forms, so that in all things you will be praised and receive glory. (1 Peter 4:10–11)

❧

Show _____ how to use her gifts and talents wisely, being faithful with the abilities you have given her. (Matthew 25:21)

❧

Thank you for the special gift you have given _____. Show him how his gift differs from the gifts you have given others, and let him be generous, diligent, and cheerful in using it. (Romans 12:6–8)

❧

*L*et _____ use her gifts for the common good, recognizing how she fits into the body of Christ and using her special abilities to build up and complement others. *(1 Corinthians 12:7–26)*

∾

*Y*ou made some people apostles, some prophets, some evangelists, and some pastors and teachers. Show _____ where he fits into your divine arrangement, and let him use his gifts to prepare your people for works of service, so that the body of Christ may be built up in love. *(Ephesians 4:11–16)*

∾

*L*et _____ use her gifts and talents for your glory. *(1 Corinthians 10:31)*

∾

*C*ause _____ to be diligent in developing his gifts and talents so that he will become "skilled in his work" and "serve before kings," using his abilities to fulfill your purposes. *(Proverbs 22:29)*

∾

*G*ive _____ a sense of destiny, and show her that you set her apart and appointed her with gifts and talents even before she was born. *(Jeremiah 1:5)*

∾

As _____ considers his gifts, cause him to lean not on his own understanding, but acknowledge you in all his ways, so that you—the One who created and gifted him— will make his paths straight. (Proverbs 3:5–6)

∾

Equip _____ with everything good for doing your will. (Hebrews 13:21)

CHAPTER FOUR

PRAYING FOR YOUR CHILD TO PROMOTE GOD'S KINGDOM

You are the light of the world.
—Matthew 5:14

FRIDAY MORNINGS ARE A HIGHLIGHT OF MY WEEK. THAT'S WHEN I get together with several moms to pray for our children, their teachers, and our school community. In addition to interceding for our kids' individual needs, we use a different verse from the Bible each week as the basis for a more general prayer that can apply to each of our children.

One morning, our collective scriptural request was for our children to have boldness in evangelism, being alert to opportunities to share the gospel with their peers. Being part of a public school community, we recognized the need for sensitivity in this area, yet we knew that God could provide open doors. We prayed according to Ephesians 5:15–16, that our kids would be very careful how they lived—not as unwise but as wise, making the most of every opportunity.

Two or three weeks went by, during which time we moved on to new requests, tucking the evangelism thoughts into the back of our minds. Then one morning Callie walked in, her face flushed with excitement. "Remember when we prayed for our kids to have boldness in evangelism and be alert to opportunities to share their faith?" she asked. "Well, listen to this . . ."

Callie began her story by reminding us about a second grader named Eddie, whose misbehavior was almost legendary in our school. We had all heard of Eddie—the tales our kids brought home tended to catapult Eddie to the top of our prayer lists, and those of us who had spent volunteer hours in Eddie's classroom knew, firsthand, how disruptive he could be. Thinking of Eddie, we often prayed that God would give his teacher, Miss Harrison, an extra measure of wisdom, patience, and love.

Many of the children instinctively tried to put some distance between themselves and Eddie, but Callie's son, Brandon, took a different approach. He befriended the boy, inviting him to be involved in games and on playground teams where he might otherwise have been left out. And one day when Miss Harrison asked each child, as an in-class assignment, to write a letter to someone, Brandon chose to write to Eddie.

When the time came for the children to deliver the letters, those who had written to parents, grandparents, or neighbors put their notes in their backpacks to take home. Brandon simply dropped his envelope on Eddie's desk. Eddie opened the letter with excitement, but when he took out the sheet of paper, his face fell. Eddie couldn't read well enough to get beyond the first few words.

Recognizing the problem but not wanting to draw attention to it, Brandon quietly asked Miss Harrison if he could read the letter aloud to Eddie.

Miss Harrison just happened to love God—and Eddie—as much as Brandon did. "Yes," she said. "You can read it to him today at recess."

That afternoon, the two boys sat on a log under the shade of an old oak tree, oblivious to the noisy shouts and energetic games being played all around them. Eddie pulled the letter out of his pocket and, leaning closer so he could hear, waited for Brandon to read it.

> *Dear Eddie,*
>
> *Please, please ask Jesus to come into your heart. Here are some reasons why:*
> *1. Jesus died on the cross for your sins.*
> *2. You will have eternal life.*
> *3. God (Jesus' father) is maker and creator of all.*
> *4. You will go to heaven.*
> *5. You can have anything you want in heaven.*
> *6. I will be waiting for you.*
> *7. God will be waiting for you.*
> *8. Jesus will be waiting for you.*
> *9. You can do anything in heaven.*
>
> *P.S. All you have to do is right now bow your head and say "dear Lord, I want Jesus to come into my heart so I can have eternal life." Amen.*

Eddie leaned back, reflecting on Brandon's words. "Would you," Brandon asked cautiously, "like to pray and ask Jesus to live in your heart right now?"

Eddie met his friend's eyes. "Yes," he said softly.

Sitting together at the edge of the playground, the two boys bowed their heads in prayer as Brandon led Eddie into the kingdom of God.

When Callie finished her story, most of us had tears in our eyes—both because of the miracle that had happened in Eddie's life and because of God's incredible faithfulness in responding so quickly to our prayers for our own children to boldly and effectively promote God's kingdom (not to mention his goodness in placing Eddie and Brandon in a class with a Christian teacher!).

In the remainder of this book, we'll focus on praying for your child's character, safety, relationships, and future. As I write this, I am reminded of how intertwined these areas are, and how each of them serves to equip us to promote God's kingdom: Brandon's kind and gentle *character,* formed in the *safety* and security of resting in Almighty God, allowed him to befriend Eddie, while his *relationships* with his parents, his peers, and his teacher paved the way for him to share the gospel. I can only imagine what the *future* holds for this exceptional young man!

Prayer Principle _____

When you pray for your children—in everything from their character to their future—you invite God to strengthen and equip them to promote his kingdom.

Prepare Yourself for God's Answer

Of course, when we pray that our children would proclaim the gospel, we open the door to a host of other factors—some of which no mother would actually *choose* for her child. We cannot see the future, and we do not know how God will answer our prayers. Perhaps God will shape our children into skilled business leaders who can give generous financial support to his work. Perhaps he will cause them to experience sickness or tragedy so that they can minister with compassion where others have no capacity to understand. Maybe he will send them overseas to some far-off country where the gospel has never been heard.

Hudson Taylor, the first Christian missionary to take the message of the gospel to inland China, is one of my father's heroes. My siblings and I grew up hearing exciting tales about Taylor's life, and when my own children learned to read, I bought them a biography that detailed his adventures. The book told of his passion for learning Chinese and sharing Christ with a people whose language and customs he could barely comprehend. It also told of the hardships and pain he faced, including the loss of his wife and three of his children.

What struck me even more than these difficulties, though, was a short paragraph recounting Taylor's departure from England at the age of twenty-one:

> His full heart almost broke at the sight of his mother standing on the pier waving good-bye. She had come aboard to be sure his cabin was adequate, and together they had sung a hymn and knelt in prayer. And then she

had returned to the pier while he remained on board. Not until the very moment of parting from his family did Hudson understand the price they were all paying by his obedience to God's call.[1]

When Hudson Taylor left for China, his family didn't know whether they would ever see him again. The journey by ship was perilous, taking six months to complete. Would I be willing to say good-bye to my son or one of my daughters, never knowing if I would see him or her again? Would I be willing—cheerfully, peacefully, wholeheartedly willing—to let them work or minister where their lives or those of their children might be at risk?

I truly hope so. I love the way another mother expressed her feelings on this subject more than a hundred years ago. Annie Rossell Fraser had prayed that at least one of her children would become a missionary, and when her son Jim left to begin working with Hudson Taylor's organization in the faraway mountains of inland China, she felt a mixture of heartache and joy. She knew she would miss him deeply, but, as the story is told in the book *Behind the Ranges*, she sent him away with a willing heart, knowing that her loneliness was for Christ's sake. "I could not pour the ointment on his blessed feet, as Mary did," she said. "But I gave him my boy."[2]

What a wonderful perspective! *Lord, make my heart like this mother's, so that nothing—from the fear of sickness or death to the threat of ostracism from their peers—will hinder my willingness to pray faithfully for my children to proclaim and promote your kingdom.*

Prayer Principle _____

> When you pray for your children to promote God's kingdom,
> you must be prepared to let them respond to his call—even if
> it means incurring risk or making great sacrifices.

_____ ∾

Poised for Prayer

In addition to praying Scriptures for my children, I like to reflect on the "heroes" of the Bible and pray that my kids will have similar strengths and attributes. In fact, when I read about particular characters in Scripture, I often make a list of the attributes they possessed that allowed them to be effective in ministry, and I ask God to shape my children's lives with similar traits.

As you pray for your children's role in promoting God's kingdom, consider asking God to give them the boldness of Paul, who was never ashamed of the gospel but saw it as a power that could not be contained. Or how about the courage of Esther, who risked her life to intercede on behalf of her people. Or the passion of King David, whose wholehearted devotion revealed him as a man after God's own heart.

We can pray, too, that our children will have the spiritual sensitivity of Stephen, a man full of wisdom, grace, and power. We can ask God to give them the out-on-a-limb faithfulness of Noah, who built an ark before anyone had even seen a raindrop ... the obedience of Abraham, who was willing to slay his own son at God's command ... the moral purity of Daniel, whose refusal to compromise his beliefs set the stage for an undeniable miracle ... or the loyalty of Ruth, who exchanged her pagan heritage for a place in the lineage of Christ.

As the Bible clearly shows, God uses all kinds of people to further his kingdom. Each of the traits I've mentioned—and so many more—can help pave the way for effective evangelism. If you like the idea of praying for your children with biblical characters in mind, I've included more information on this strategy in the appendix ("Using Biblical Characters to Pray for Your Children").

As we pray, let's ask God, above all else, to fill our children with the heart and mind of Christ, with the result that they might reach out to others with his life-changing love.

Prayers You Can Use

Heavenly Father...

Let _____'s light shine before others, that they may see his good deeds and praise you, our Father in heaven. (Matthew 5:16)

∾

I pray that _____ would always be prepared to give an answer to everyone who asks her to give the reason for the *hope that she has, and cause her to speak with gentleness and respect. (1 Peter 3:15)*

∾

Let _____ sing of your great love forever; let him make known your faithfulness through all generations. (Psalm 89:1)

∾

May _____ never be ashamed of the gospel, but let her recognize that it is the power of God for the salvation of everyone who believes. (Romans 1:16)

∾

I pray that _____ would go and make disciples of all nations, baptizing them in the name of the Father and of the Son and of the Holy Spirit, and teaching them to obey everything you have commanded us. (The Great Commission, Matthew 28:19–20)

∾

Cause _____ to follow you, and make him a fisher of people. (Matthew 4:19)

∾

*L*et _____ become blameless and pure, a child of God without fault in a crooked and depraved generation, and let _____ shine like a star in the universe as she holds out the word of life. (Philippians 2:15–16)

ॐ

*W*henever _____ opens his mouth, give him the words to say so that he will fearlessly make known the mystery of the gospel. (Ephesians 6:19)

ॐ

*F*ill _____ with the knowledge of your will through all spiritual wisdom and understanding, so that she may live a life worthy of you and may please you in every way: bearing fruit in every good work and growing in the knowledge of you, Lord. (Colossians 1:9–10)

ॐ

*L*et _____ preach the word and be prepared, in season and out of season; let him correct, rebuke, and encourage— with great patience and careful instruction. When the time comes that people do not put up with sound doctrine but listen to teachers who say what their itching ears want to hear, don't let _____ lose heart. Let him keep his head in all situations, endure hardship, and do the work of an evangelist. (2 Timothy 4:2–5)

Part Two

Praying for Your Child's Character

CHAPTER FIVE

PRAYING FOR WISDOM AND DISCERNMENT

If any of you lacks wisdom, he should ask God,
who gives generously to all without finding fault,
and it will be given to him.

—James 1:5

"CAN ANNESLEY COME OVER RIGHT NOW AND PLAY WITH Christopher?"

I smiled when I heard the urgency in my friend Nancy's voice. "Sure," I replied. "But what's the rush?"

"Well," Nancy explained, "Christopher was supposed to play at a friend's house this afternoon, but when he got there, his buddy wanted to watch some horror movie. Christopher said he didn't think that was a good idea, and that his mom wouldn't let him."

"And?" I said, laughing. "*Would* you have let him?"

"Of course not—but that's not the point. Christopher kept saying he wasn't going to watch the movie, and his friend kept insisting he should, until finally the friend's mom heard the boys arguing and asked what the problem was. When the guys told her what was up, she got mad at her kid and sent Christopher home. So now he has nothing to do this afternoon—all because he made a wise choice!

"And so," Nancy finished, "I want to reward him. Christopher always enjoys Annesley's company . . . and if it's okay with you, I'll come pick her up right now."

It wasn't until after I had hung up the phone that it hit me: Nancy is one of the leaders of our Friday morning prayer group, and we had recently prayed for our children according to Philippians 1:9–10, that they might have "knowledge and depth of insight" and be able to "discern what is best" and be "pure and blameless until the day of Christ." Talk about an answer to prayer!

Christopher's refusal to watch the horror movie might seem like a decision of little consequence—and in fact, he might not even remember making the choice in years to come. But as he continues to mature, such wisdom and discernment will make all the difference in how effectively he responds to life's circumstances.

Just how important is wisdom? Proverbs 4:7 says that wisdom is "supreme," and that understanding is worth whatever it costs to get it. Ecclesiastes 7:11–12 likens wisdom to money, but notes that wisdom is the superior asset because it "preserves the life of its possessor." And when King Solomon asked God to give him wisdom, he got a whole lot more than he bargained for.

Perhaps you recall the story: The Lord had offered to give Solomon anything he wanted. Recognizing the challenges associated with the kingship, Solomon asked for "a discerning heart," that he might govern wisely and be able to distinguish between right and wrong.

The Lord was obviously pleased with Solomon's request. "Since you have asked for this and not for long life or wealth for yourself," he said, "I will do what you have asked. I will give you a wise and discerning heart, so that there will never have been anyone like you, nor will there ever be." And the Lord wasn't finished. "Moreover," he continued, "I will give you what you have not asked for—both riches and honor—so that in your lifetime you will have no equal among kings. And if you walk in my ways and obey my statutes and commands as David your father did, I will give you a long life."[1] When Solomon asked God for wisdom, God gave it to him, along with an incredible array of other blessings.

Prayer Principle

> Asking God to give your children wisdom is asking him to equip them to receive every other blessing he wants to provide.

Choosing the Best over the Good

When Jesus wanted to give his disciples nuggets of wisdom, he often used stories, parables, and questions to pique their curiosity. As a mother, I find such curiosity-piquers almost everywhere I look—even when I'd rather not notice them.

For instance, our older girls are avid readers. Sometimes, though, they come home from school with books that I'd have preferred they had left on the shelf. A year or so ago they brought home a paperback from a series that was very popular with their classmates. Having heard less-than-rave reviews from a friend whose counsel I value highly, I decided to give the book a quick skim. There was nothing overtly wrong with it—no offensive words, no occultish stuff, no violence to speak of—but I didn't especially like its tone.

"Well?" the girls asked when I closed the cover. "Can we read it?"

"Yes," I replied, thinking of how Jesus used curiosity as a teaching tool. "You can read it—on one condition. When you are finished, I want you to give me a book report. I want to know three things about the book that make you think it is good, or three things that make you think it isn't."

It wasn't long before I got some answers. "Well," Annesley offered, "the girl hides books and candy under her bed so her mom won't find them. That's not good."

"And," Hillary put in, "she calls a boy in her class a jerk."

"Mm-hmm," I said. "Anything else?"

The girls threw out a few more ideas, most of which pertained to character deficits in the story's characters. They failed to notice that the book wasn't even very interesting or well-written, but I let that slide. "So what's the verdict?" I asked.

"It's okay," they concluded. "But it's not as good as we thought it would be."

That was putting it nicely. My friend Kenzie likes to quote 1 Corinthians 10:23 to her kids: "'Everything is permissible'—but not everything is beneficial." As I talked with the girls about the book, I was reminded of another of Kenzie's maxims: "With so many great books to choose from, why should our kids waste their time on anything that isn't really good?"

Why indeed? God wants the best for our children. Why should we—or they—settle for anything less? We won't always be around to screen the books our kids read or the movies they watch, or influence our kids with respect to the companions they choose or the job offers they accept. But God will. So, as we pray for our children now and in the future, let's ask God to give them a wise and discerning heart, along with a passion for pursuing his very best.

Prayer Principle

> Praying for your children to desire God's best will help prevent them from settling for that which is merely adequate or good.

Looking at Life through God's Eyes

One of my favorite prayers for my children (and for my husband, Robbie, for that matter) is the apostle Paul's prayer in Colossians 1:9–12. Paul writes these beautiful words:

We have not stopped praying for you and asking God to fill you with the knowledge of his will through all spiritual wisdom and understanding. . . . that you may live a life worthy of the Lord and may please him in every way: bearing fruit in every good work, growing in the knowledge of God, being strengthened with all power according to his glorious might so that you may have great endurance and patience, and joyfully giving thanks to the Father, who has qualified you to share in the inheritance of the saints in the kingdom of light.

In her excellent Bible study book titled *Becoming a Woman of Prayer,* Cynthia Heald quotes author C. Samuel Storms on the subject of this prayer:

Paul did not pray that [the Colossians] be spared suffering. Nor did he request that material wealth be added to their spiritual zeal. He said nothing about illness, or healing, or better jobs, or any of those things for which we pray and ask others to pray on our behalf. Such requests are not always inappropriate, but we see that Paul considered spiritual wisdom, knowledge, and enlightenment of greater value.[2]

What is it about wisdom and enlightenment that make them so very valuable? Eugene Peterson, in his contemporary English version of the Colossians passage, offers a clue: "We haven't stopped praying for you," Peterson's translation reads, "asking God to give you wise minds and spirits attuned to his will, and so acquire a thorough understanding of the ways in which God works."[3] The reason godly wisdom is so important is that it opens our minds to the way God works and allows us to respond to life with God's perspective.

My friend Lanie has always prayed that her children will have wisdom, and not long ago, God treated her to a glimpse of how he has answered her prayers. She and her husband, Tim, had been house-hunting and thought they had found the perfect home. As it turned out, someone else must have liked the house too, because before Tim and Lanie knew what was happening, the house had been sold.

Apparently, one of the real estate agents involved in the deal had worked things so that Tim and Lanie were unable to bid on the house in time, and Tim was miffed. Driving down the road, he struggled to conceal his irritation from their ten-year-old son, Tyson. But then Tyson said something that stopped Tim's anger dead in its tracks. "I know you and Mom really liked that house, Dad," he said. "But I guess that's a 'no' from the Lord."

Tyson looked at the situation through God's eyes—and in doing so, he saw something that his father had missed. Wisdom had opened Tyson's eyes to God's answer.

Prayer Principle

When you ask God to give your children wisdom and discernment, you are asking him to enable them to see the world through his eyes—and to think, speak, act, and respond accordingly.

Poised for Prayer

When we ask God to give our children wisdom and discernment, we aren't just asking him to help them make right choices. We are setting them up for a lifetime of intimacy with Christ, "in whom are hidden all the treasures of wisdom and knowledge."[4] And the spillover effect from this type of relationship can be invaluable. Consider just a few of the things that wisdom can do for our kids:

- It helps them manage their time effectively (Psalm 90:12).
- It makes them good listeners (Proverbs 1:5).
- It provides direction and purpose in life (Proverbs 3:5–6).
- It opens the door to happiness, true riches, and a long and pleasant life (Proverbs 3:13–17).
- It offers insight into the character of others and protection from evil (Proverbs 7:4–5).
- It leads to strong, joy-filled family relationships (Proverbs 10:1).
- It even makes them *look* better (Ecclesiastes 8:1).

Eugene Peterson sums up wisdom as "the art of living skillfully in whatever conditions we find ourselves."[5] To learn more about the art of skillful living and the rewards God offers to wisdom seekers, dip into the Old Testament's treasure chest of wisdom, the book of Proverbs. With thirty-one chapters, Proverbs makes a great one-a-day monthly Bible study or family devotional guide. Read it with your kids—and then turn its wisdom-laden verses into power-filled prayers.

Prayers You Can Use

Heavenly Father...

Fill _____ with the knowledge of your will through all spiritual wisdom and understanding, that he might live a life worthy of you, Lord, and please you in every way. (Colossians 1:9–10)

Give _____ wisdom. Thank you that you give generously to everyone without finding fault. Help _____ to believe and not doubt, and give her singleness of mind and stability in all that she does. Help her to be decisive and to make good decisions. (James 1:5–8)

Cause _____ to fear you, since this is the beginning of wisdom. Cause _____ to know you, and to understand your perspective on any situation. Add years to his life, and give him the reward of the wise. (Proverbs 9:10–12)

Do not let _____ look at the things man looks at, but let her see the world through your eyes and respond to it with your wisdom and your love. (1 Samuel 16:7)

73

∾

Give _____ wisdom and understanding. Do not let him forget your words or swerve from them. Cause him to love wisdom and to value it above all worldly desires and accomplishments. (Proverbs 4:5–7)

∾

Let _____ trust in you with all her heart. Don't let her rely on her own understanding, but cause her to acknowledge you in all her ways, and make her paths straight. (Proverbs 3:5–6)

∾

Counsel _____, Lord. Instruct him, even during the night. Make known to him the path of life and fill him with joy in your presence. (Psalm 16:7, 11)

∾

Give _____ a wise and discerning heart so that she can distinguish between right and wrong. (1 Kings 3:9, 12)

∾

Let your Spirit rest on _____. Give him the Spirit of wisdom and understanding, the Spirit of counsel and power, the Spirit of knowledge and of the fear of the Lord—that he might delight in the fear of the Lord. Don't let _____ *judge by what he sees with his eyes, or decide by what he hears with his ears, but let him act with righteousness, justice, and faith. (Isaiah 11:2–5)*

∾

This is my prayer: that _____ 's love may abound more and more in knowledge and depth of insight, so that she may be able to discern what is best and may be pure and blameless until the day of Christ, filled with the fruit of righteousness that comes through Jesus Christ. (Philippians 1:9–11)

CHAPTER SIX

PRAYING FOR A SERVANT'S HEART

Let us not become weary in doing good, for at the proper time we will reap a harvest if we do not give up.

—Galatians 6:9

WHEN OUR CHILDREN WERE IN PRESCHOOL, THE SCHOOL NURSE used to push a snack cart—loaded with treats that measured up to her strict nutritional standards—from classroom to classroom each morning. She genuinely loved the kids and her job, so I was surprised to see her storming down the hall one day, her face flushed with indignation.

"What's wrong?" I asked.

"One of the children just called me her *servant!*" she exploded. "I didn't know how to respond!"

I felt my eyes light up as I burst into laughter. "A servant!" I exclaimed. "I can't think of a higher compliment!"

Bewildered, the nurse stared at me for a long moment before moving on down the hall, again at a loss for words. She may have thought I was nuts, but at least she didn't say so. Not that I would have blamed her if she had. These days, nobody wants to be thought of as a "servant." We may say (and even think) that serving others is important, but our actions and priorities send a different message. Whether we are in the grocery store checkout line or the office conference room, we find ourselves jockeying for position, striving for control, eager to be first. And, in a culture that rarely notices or rewards selflessness, you have to wonder whether cultivating a servant's heart is all that important. Is it really worth praying for?

Jesus certainly thought so. In fact, he put his personal stamp of approval on servanthood, telling his disciples that "whoever wants to become great among you must be your servant, and whoever wants to be first must be your slave—just as the Son of Man did not come to be served, but to serve, and to give his life as a ransom for many."[1]

Jesus came to serve, even to the point of giving his life. Praying for a servant's heart, then, is akin to asking God to make our children more like Christ.

Prayer Principle _____

When you ask God to give your child a servant's heart, you are praying that he or she will be like Jesus.

_____ ❧

What's in It for You?

It was shaping up to be one of the worst snowstorms Susan could remember. As she drove her station wagon through the barely visible streets of their Washington, D.C.–area neighborhood, she prayed they would make it home safely. Three of her five children were buckled into the backseat, and getting stranded in one of Washington's infamous blizzards held very little appeal.

As Susan approached a bend in the road, she could see the hulking forms of three or four cars that had slid off the road and into a ditch. She could feel the icy conditions beneath her wheels and slowed the car to a crawl. Drawing abreast of the disabled cars, she was surprised to see a group of teenage boys struggling to push one of the cars back onto the road, seemingly oblivious to the biting wind.

"Look, Mom!" ten-year-old Chris cried. "Those guys must be freezing!"

"Yeah," agreed twelve-year-old John, "but just think of how much money they're making!"

Susan and her kids watched the teenagers pool their strength in one final heave. As the car inched its way back onto the road, the teens lifted their arms in triumph and then turned their attention to the next stranded vehicle.

"Could it be," Susan asked quietly, "that these guys are not out here to make money? Could it be that they just want to help people get their cars out of the ditch?"

The boys hadn't considered this possibility, but as they continued to watch the rescue operation, they had to admit that their mother was probably right. No money changed hands, but as the teens worked to free each car from its snowy bondage, their enthusiasm seemed to grow. Their reward, it appeared, was bound up in the task at hand.

Seminar speaker Bill Gothard says that having a servant's heart means you get excited about making someone else successful.[2] Heartfelt service, in other words, goes beyond merely *rejoicing* when another person succeeds; it involves *taking action* that contributes to the victory. It involves more than just cheerleading; it involves giving up your warm, comfortable seat by the fire and venturing out into a blinding snowstorm to push a bunch of stranded cars out of the ditch.

Scripture tells the story of another teenager who gave up his comfortable position in order to work on behalf of someone else. Jonathan, King Saul's oldest son, stood to inherit the kingdom of Israel. The only thing standing between him and the kingship was a little-known shepherd-turned-giant-killer named David, whose battlefield triumphs eventually won the heart of a nation. With his father bent on murdering David, Jonathan could have stayed on the sideline, trying on crowns and brushing up on his foreign policy. Instead, he risked his life—and ultimately, his dynasty—to orchestrate David's escape and help pave the way for David to take over the kingdom.[3]

Jonathan, the Bible tells us, loved David as he loved himself.[4] It's that kind of love that will compel our children to give up their "crowns"—their rights, their positions, their time—in order to help other people. Jesus made the connection between love and sacrificial service in John 15:12–13: "Love each other as I have loved you. Greater love has no one than this, that he lay down his life for his friends." With these words in mind, let's ask God to let our children be motivated by love, so that they can be genuinely excited about serving others—even if it means sacrificing their own needs or desires.

Prayer Principle _____

> Praying for a servant's heart involves praying
> for genuine, self-sacrificing love.

_____ ❧

"Everyday" Service

We've all read stories about modern heroes who have risked their lives to pull people from burning cars, rescue flood victims from drowning, and even shield children from bullets. We praise and honor these acts of service. For most of us, though, opportunities for such valiant behavior are few and far between. For most of us, "giving our lives" involves little more than making lunches or participating in car pools. For our kids, letting a sibling have the front seat in the car, mowing the grass for the single mom who lives next door, or pushing a few cars out of a snowdrift may be as heroic as life gets. In God's grand scheme, do these little "everyday" things count?

Yes. Yes, absolutely! Anytime we put other's needs and desires ahead of our own, speaking or acting on someone else's behalf, we give up our lives—our time, our talents, our resources, our "rights"—and follow Christ's call to service.

Monica is always on the lookout for ways to encourage her children (all eleven of them!) in this area. Once, when her eight-year-old daughter wanted to bake and deliver a pie to their elderly housekeeper, Monica found herself driving all the way across town at dinnertime—in Atlanta's notorious rush-hour traffic—just so the little girl could deliver her gift, along with a hug. As it turned out, it was the last visit they had with their housekeeper. She died not long afterwards, and this simple act of service turned into a cherished memory that Monica and her daughter will never forget.

Did it make sense for Monica to pile her kids into the car during rush hour in a big city? No, not really. But opportunities for service don't always come in tidy little packages or at convenient times. Think of how the Virgin Mary must have felt when the angel told her the news: You will give birth to the Son of God. Had I been in Mary's sandals, I probably would have protested vigorously at this incredible invasion of my privacy . . . this upsetting of my schedule . . . this unexpected kink in my wedding plans. But Mary took the news in stride. Luke 1:38 records her simple answer: "I am the Lord's *servant*. . . . May it be to me as you have said" (emphasis added).

It was not convenient for Monica to make an impromptu pie delivery—any more than it fit into Mary's plans to get pregnant before she was married. But by following the promptings of a servant's heart, both women reaped an unexpected and wonderful blessing.

As we pray for our children, then, let's not place limits on how or where we want them to serve, or on what we expect them to do. Instead, let's keep watch for signs of a servant's heart, and, as we see it budding, let's pray according to Colossians 3:23–24: "Whatever you do, work at it with all your heart, as working for the Lord, not for men, since you know that you will receive an inheritance from the Lord as a reward. It is the Lord Christ you are serving."

"Whatever you do, work at it with all your heart, *as working for the Lord*." This emphasis on the "Who" rather than on the "what" can be a terrific motivator, particularly when the job to be done is not particularly glamorous. Something as seemingly inconsequential as making a sibling's bed or carrying groceries into the house from the car can take on a new luster when it is done in the service of the King of kings. Remind your kids—again and again—that when they serve others, they are serving the Lord.

Prayer Principle _____

> Praying for your children to develop a servant's heart means praying that they will learn to look beyond the task at hand to see the Master whom they serve.

Poised for Prayer

Not all acts of service will be truly helpful—especially when your children are young. Just last week Hillary and Annesley unloaded the dishwasher and put everything away for me. I hadn't asked them to do this, and I was grateful for their thoughtfulness. The only problem was that the dishwasher hadn't been run yet and the dishes were still dirty.

At times like these, it helps to remember that *attitude* is more important than *accomplishment*. Philippians 2:5–7 underscores this lesson. "Your attitude should be the same as that of Christ Jesus," Paul writes, pointing out that Christ "made himself nothing, taking the very nature of a servant." Notice that Paul doesn't say our *accomplishments* should be the same as those of Christ Jesus. Rather, he focuses on our *attitude*.

Attitudes you can pray for that translate into effective service include things like kindness, compassion, generosity, and self-lessness. I also pray that my children will be alert and diligent, willing to go the extra mile to see a project through to completion. The verse I cite at the very beginning of this chapter is one of my all-time favorites: "Let us not become weary in doing good, for at the proper time we will reap a harvest if we do not give up." I pray this verse for my kids, counting on God to open their eyes to opportunities for service. I pray this for their teachers, knowing how much they need an extra dose of strength, energy, and hope. And I pray it for myself, banking on *Jehovah Elohim*—literally, the Lord who is both personal and almighty, both willing and able, both loving and powerful—to sustain me through the challenges of raising four children and pointing them toward Christ—even when they stock my cupboards with dirty dishes.

Prayers You Can Use

Heavenly Father...

Don't let _____ become weary in doing good. Let him know that at the proper time he will reap a harvest if he does not give up. (Galatians 6:9)

∽

Thank you that _____ is your workmanship, created in Christ Jesus to do good works, which you prepared in advance for her to do. (Ephesians 2:10)

∽

Let _____ do nothing out of selfish ambition or vain conceit, but in humility consider others better than himself. Let him look not only to his own interests, but also to the interests of others, and let his attitude be the same as that of Christ Jesus. (Philippians 2:3–5)

∽

Let _____ worship and serve others in love. (Galatians 5:13)

∽

Whatever _____ does, let her work at it with all her heart, as working for you, not for people. (Colossians 3:23)

∽

Let _____ worship and serve you with gladness. (Psalm 100:2)

❧

*M*otivate _____ to serve wholeheartedly, as if he were serving you, not people, and remind him that you will reward everyone for whatever good they do. (Ephesians 6:7–8)

❧

*T*each _____ that if she wants to become great, she must be a servant. If she wants to be first, she must be a slave— just as the Son of Man did not come to be served, but to serve, and to give his life as a ransom for many. (Matthew 20:26–28)

❧

*A*bove all, let _____ love others deeply, because love covers over a multitude of sins. Let _____ use whatever gift he has received to serve others, faithfully administering your grace in its various forms. Let him serve with the strength you provide, so that in all things you, O Lord, will get the credit and the glory. (1 Peter 4:8–11)

CHAPTER SEVEN

PRAYING FOR KINDNESS AND COMPASSION

Therefore, as God's chosen people, holy and dearly loved, clothe yourselves with compassion, kindness, humility, gentleness and patience.

—Colossians 3:12

"I'M SORRY, CLASS," THE TEACHER SAID, "BUT WE CAN'T GO OUTside. It's nearly freezing out there, and Bryant hasn't brought a coat or anything warm to wear."

Amid the chorus of groans and protests, Will looked across the room at the fifth grader who sat hunched at his desk, clad only in shorts and a T-shirt. Bryant never complained—in fact, he never said much of anything—but Will figured his classmate *had* to be cold. It was January, and ice from a recent storm still clung in stubborn patches to the grass and sidewalks around the school. Why didn't the boy have the sense to wear some pants, or a sweater at least?

"Thanks a lot, Bryant!" another boy hissed. "This is the third day we've had to miss recess. Why don't you do us all a favor and just stay home tomorrow?"

Bryant kept silent, his eyes focused on his desk. Will turned his attention to the window. He could see the basketball court outside, smooth and dry in the winter sunshine. Even in the cold, it looked inviting. Maybe Bryant would stay home. Then they could all go out and play. Or maybe Bryant would wake up and realize that it was cold outside. Maybe he would wear something warmer.

That night, as Will sat at the kitchen table doing his homework, his thoughts returned to the classroom. "Mom, do you think that Bryant might not *have* any warm clothes?"

"Who's Bryant?"

"This kid in my class. He wears shorts every day, and Mrs. Cooper said we can't go outside unless everyone wears something warm." Will thought for a minute. "Could I bring him some of my clothes?"

Katherine turned and smiled at her oldest child. "Sure, honey. That would be nice."

But Will wasn't finished. "I'd better not bring anything big—I wouldn't want him to think that I thought he was poor or something. Maybe just some pants, at least at first. And Mom?" he added. "Could we pray for Bryant? I really don't want to offend him."

Katherine put down the dish towel she had been holding and gave her son a hug. Silently, she thanked God for giving Will such a kind and sensitive spirit, and then the two of them prayed together for Bryant's receptivity to Will's offer.

The next day Will took an extra pair of pants to school. Eager to hear how the exchange went, Katherine met her son at the door when he came home.

"What did Bryant say?" she asked.

"He said 'Thanks,'" Will replied matter-of-factly. "And Mom, I told him not to worry if he tore the pants or anything. I said he could just give them back and we would fix them."

Katherine laughed and tousled Will's hair. *"We?"*

Will scampered out of reach and started up the stairs. Suddenly, he stopped and turned. "Um," he said sheepishly, "I mean *you*. You would fix them if they got torn ... wouldn't you?"

I love this story for what it teaches us about cultivating kindness and compassion in our children. First, it reminds us to pray specifically for our kids to recognize and seize the opportunity to care for others, even in the face of uncertainty or difficulty. After all, there is always the risk that kindness will go unappreciated: As Will noted, Bryant could easily have rebuffed his overture.

Additionally, we need to pray that our children will identify with the needs of those around them, remembering that it could just as easily be one of *them* who was hurting. As Hebrews 13:3 puts it, "Remember those in prison as if you were their fellow prisoners, and those who are mistreated as if you yourselves were suffering."

Prayer Principle _____

When you pray that your children will be alert to opportunities to show kindness and compassion, you invite God to help them slip into other people's shoes.

Christlike Compassion: The Genuine Article

John Yates, rector of The Falls Church (Episcopal) in Falls Church, Virginia, says that compassion is "having pity, feeling sympathy for another, and doing something about it."[1] But this combination of *attitude* and *action* does not always come easily, particularly in our self-centered, fast-paced society.

The chart I once posted on our refrigerator is a case in point. I listed a number of character traits down the left-hand side of the chart—compassion, self-control, generosity, and the like—and wrote each of our names across the top. The idea was to focus on a different trait each week, awarding stars as folks demonstrated the various attributes. The only restriction I placed on the game was that you couldn't acknowledge your own good behavior; someone else had to point it out.

I never should have put compassion first. After about four days I couldn't help but notice that my kids were collecting stars left and right, and even Dad had a few in his column. My own column, however, was totally blank. According to the chart, I had a heart of steel.

I tried to convince myself that the problem lay in my kids' inability to recognize their mother's virtues, but, looking back over the preceding days, I had to admit that the chart was right. My day was so packed with laundry, car pools, and other mundane stuff that, as I raced from one commitment or activity to the next, I had neither the time nor the inclination to be compassionate. I was, I realized with a guilty jolt, one of the "bad" guys in the parable of the Good Samaritan.[2] Like them, I ignored the needs of the folks in my path, giving hurting or emotionally wounded people a wide berth so their problems wouldn't derail my "agenda."

I had a hard heart. And what was worse, I was modeling it for my children—with the irrefutable evidence of my un-starred glory blazing on the refrigerator door for all to see.

Having been made aware of my shortcomings, I decided to "fix" them. I purposed to show compassion at every turn. When my children fell down, I slathered them with hugs and kisses. When they had trouble at school, I lent a sympathetic ear and tried to look like I felt their pain. When the church called to see if we would "adopt" a lonely college student, I readily agreed. "Yes!" I said with great enthusiasm. "In fact, we'll take two!"

"Mom," ten-year-old Hillary observed at last, as I tried (rather forcefully) to fold her lanky frame onto my lap after she had skinned her knee on our neighbor's basketball court, "I think you're overdoing it. *That* is not real compassion. In fact, the way you're holding me kind of hurts."

Ouch. Hillary was right. In my feeble attempt to manufacture a compassionate heart, I had replaced the genuine article with gushy sentimentalism and insincerity. I was exercising counterfeit compassion, and it wasn't doing anybody any good.

In an effort to discover what I was missing, I looked up the word *compassion* in a concordance. There were no less than 120 references, and I read each verse in which the word appears. In the Old Testament, the picture emerges again and again of a compassionate father-figure, a God whose "compassions never fail."[3] In the New Testament, this same compassion seemed to be what motivated Jesus to stop, to listen, to touch, and to heal—over and over again.

As I wrestled with how to appropriate God's compassion and follow Christ's example, I happened upon 1 John 3:17–18: "If anyone has material possessions and sees his brother in need but has no pity on him, how can the love of God be in him? Dear children, let us not love with words or tongue but with actions and in truth."

Wrapped up in these verses are the ingredients that mark genuine kindness and compassion: A readiness to share, an ability to recognize needs, a sympathetic heart, an openness to God's love, and a willingness to take action on behalf of others. These are the characteristics that marked Jesus' ministry on earth, and they are the ones I pray will mark our children's lives.

Prayer Principle

Praying for your children's lives to be marked with a Christlike compassion opens the door for God to work on their attitudes as well as their actions.

Walking with the King

As evidenced by my ill-fated attempts to register on the family "star" chart, it is impossible to manufacture compassion—either in ourselves or in our children. We cannot make our kids sensitive to the needs of others, we cannot compel them to feel pity or love, and we cannot force them to translate these attitudes into action.

How, then, can we cultivate kindness and compassion in their hearts?

I think my grandmother had the right answer to this question. She was one of the most compassionate people I have ever known. Truth be told, Gammy's determination to exercise kindness and compassion bordered on the militant, and our family lore is brimming with tales of her unorthodox methods of "ministering" to those around her. Long before anyone had ever heard of Martin Luther King Jr., Gammy was doing her part for civil rights, startling her anti-Semitic acquaintances by proclaiming that *she* was a Jew (which she technically wasn't, but, to her way of thinking, being a child of Israel's God was close enough), and getting herself forever banned from the local country club for inviting a "dark-skinned" woman to sit with her at the garden club luncheon.

The secret to Gammy's ability to recognize needs and act on them was this: She tended to regard *everyone* she met— the good, the bad, and the ugly—as a precious child of God. Because she saw God's image reflected in those around her, she found it easy to love others and identify with their needs. She considered it a joy, rather than a burden, to devote her time, money, and energy to meeting them. And under her constant encouragement, her four children began to share her vision. "Walk with the King today," Gammy would say each morning as she sent them off to school, "and be a blessing!"

Prayer Principle _____

The most effective prayers for kindness and compassion begin with an awareness of the God-created preciousness of those in need.

Poised for Prayer

Taking a page out of Gammy's book, we can pray that our own children will walk with the King and be a blessing—even if it means putting their own needs, desires, or "agendas" on hold. We can pray that they will see Jesus reflected in their friends, their teammates, their teachers, and their family. And we can pray that they will not be hard-hearted, but that they will look at the world through heaven's loving eyes.

With this vision in mind, one of my favorite prayers comes from Ezekiel 11:19. In this verse, God tells the Israelites that he will "give them an undivided heart and put a new spirit in them" and "remove from them their heart of stone and give them a heart of flesh." God does not change: He is the same yesterday, today, and forever. What he did for the Israelites, he can do for our kids, turning hardened hearts of stone into compassionate hearts of flesh.

God is, after all, in the heart surgery business.

Prayers You Can Use

Heavenly Father...

Clothe_____ with compassion, kindness, humility, gentleness, and patience. (Colossians 3:12)

∾

*L*et _____ be kind and compassionate to others, forgiving them just as in Christ God forgave him. (Ephesians 4:32)

∾

*C*omfort _____ in all her troubles, so that she may comfort those in any trouble with the comfort she has received from you, precious Lord. (2 Corinthians 1:4)

∾

*Y*our word says that if anyone has material possessions and sees his brother in need but has no pity on him, how can the love of God be in him? Therefore, let _____ not love with mere words, but let him love others with actions and in truth. (1 John 3:17–18)

∾

*D*o not let _____ forget to entertain strangers, for by doing so some people have entertained angels without knowing it. Prompt her to remember those in prison as if she were their fellow prisoner, and those who are mistreated as if she herself were suffering. (Hebrews 13:2–3)

∾

*L*et _____ open his arms to the poor and extend his hands to the needy. (Proverbs 31:20)

❧

*T*hank you for showing compassion to us. I pray that
_____ would follow your example, being compassionate
and gracious, slow to anger, and abounding in love. *(Psalm
103:8)*

❧

*F*ill _____ with your Holy Spirit, that she might bear
the Spirit's fruit: love, joy, peace, patience, kindness, goodness, faithfulness, gentleness, and self-control. *(Galatians
5:22–23)*

❧

*L*et _____ be willing to forgive not seven times, but sev-
enty-seven times—in unlimited amounts. Let him have pity
on others, acting with patience and mercy in all things.
(Matthew 18:21–35)

CHAPTER EIGHT

PRAYING FOR SELF-CONTROL, DILIGENCE, AND SELF-DISCIPLINE

No discipline seems pleasant at the time, but painful.
Later on, however, it produces a harvest of righteousness
and peace for those who have been trained by it.

—Hebrews 12:11

MEGAN AND CHIP HAVE TWO SONS. ONE IS USUALLY CHEERFUL, docile, and eager to please. The other is often defiant, disobedient, and prone to fits of temper. Same parents—very different kids. Their situation illustrates what almost every parent knows: Some children are born with tendencies toward self-discipline and self-control, and some are not. But this doesn't mean that the "have-nots" don't need these traits or that they cannot acquire them. In fact, children who lack these attributes *must* learn them if they are to become satisfied, happy, productive adults. Consider the following warnings from the book of Proverbs:

- "Like a city whose walls are broken down is a man who lacks self-control."
- "He who guards his lips guards his life, but he who speaks rashly will come to ruin."
- "The sluggard craves and gets nothing, but the desires of the diligent are fully satisfied."
- "The evil deeds of a wicked man ensnare him; the cords of his sin hold him fast. He will die for lack of discipline, led astray by his own great folly."[1]

I don't know of any parents who would want their children compared to a city with broken-down walls. Nor can I think of anyone who would wish ruin, dissatisfaction, or death on their kids. Yet without things like self-control, diligence, and self-discipline, this is exactly what the future holds.

Do I sound like an extremist? Maybe so—but you don't need much of an imagination to envision the possibilities: The girl who fails to learn to do what's *right*—instead of what *feels good*—may one day find it relatively easy to have an affair or walk out on her husband when the going gets tough. The young man who never learns perseverance and self-discipline may eventually find himself drifting from job to job, easily dissatisfied and ready to quit when boredom sets in or the pressure starts to mount. And what's to stop the child who lacks self-control from becoming an adult who has no control over his appetite for food, money, sex, gossip, anger, or violence?

By contrast, the future looks bright for children who learn to exercise self-discipline, diligence, and self-control. Proverbs 10:4 says, "Lazy hands make a man poor, but diligent hands bring wealth." Hebrews 12:11 promises that discipline will produce "a harvest of righteousness and peace for those who have been trained by it." And 2 Peter 1:5–8 links attributes like self-control and perseverance to effective, productive Christianity.

Which do you want for your kids: Poverty, dissatisfaction, and unrest ... or wealth, righteousness, and peace? Brokenness, ruin, and death ... or effective, productive living? If you picked the latter traits, then character traits like diligence and self-control are not optional in your children's lives. They are mandatory assets without which genuine happiness, contentment, and satisfaction become impossible to attain.

Prayer Principle

> When you pray for your children to learn things like diligence and self-control, you are asking God to give them attributes that are absolutely essential to their future happiness and success.

Learn to See Trials as Teachers

Self-control, diligence, and self-discipline may open the door to happiness, but they don't always come easily. Learning these traits can be tough—on children *and* parents.

Years ago I heard author Susan Yates say that she and her friends often prayed that if their teenagers were doing anything wrong, they would be caught. Better to get nabbed at a relatively young age and learn an important lesson, they figured, than to grow up never paying the consequences—and never learning traits like self-discipline and self-control.

One of the moms in our Friday morning group didn't have to wait until her kids were teenagers to employ Yates's prayer. For several weeks her first grader had been coming home with a few "extras" in his book bag—pencils, erasers, and other classroom "treats" he claimed to have earned for his work. Sensing that something was amiss, the mother contacted the boy's teacher, who confirmed her fears: Classroom supplies were disappearing, and her son was the prime suspect! The only problem was that he had not been caught in the act— and he refused to own up to his crimes.

Most mothers (myself included) might have been tempted to sweep the incriminating facts under the rug and simply ask their friends to pray for the "difficult situation" their child was in. But not this mom. She told us exactly what was up and asked us to pray specifically that her son would be caught, that he would admit to being a liar and a thief, and that he would be sorry for his sin.

Praying for a first grader in such a bald-faced manner seemed almost funny—until I remembered what happened to a group of high schoolers whose parents chose to see their children's misbehavior in a different light. With graduation approaching, school officials had warned the students that end-of-the-year pranks would not be tolerated. Anyone caught in such mischief would not be allowed to attend the school's prom or participate in the graduation ceremonies.

Several students ignored the warnings and spread motor oil all over the school's foyer, congratulating themselves on coming up with a prank that eclipsed those of previous classes.

When they were caught, they were stunned to find out that they wouldn't be permitted to attend the year-end festivities. Disbelief quickly gave way to anger, and the prank became the talk of our town.

What surprised me more than the students' apparent disregard for the warnings they had received was their parents' reactions. Some parents agreed with the school's decision, but an amazing number rallied around their ill-behaved children, blasting school administrators and threatening all kinds of retaliation. I felt sorry for the teenagers. *Perhaps,* I thought, *if their folks had prayed for (and enforced) a dose of self-control when they pilfered pencils in elementary school, their characters would have been polished to a brighter shine when the teenage years rolled around.*

Our little first-grade thief was eventually apprehended, and he expressed genuine remorse for his actions. Reading Proverbs 19:18 ("Discipline your son, for in that there is hope; do not be a willing party to his death"), I couldn't help but admire my Friday morning friend. By praying for her son to be caught—and by using the experience to foster discipline and self-control—she gave him the priceless gifts of hope and life.

Prayer Principle _____

Praying for God to give your children things like diligence, self-discipline, and a sense of responsibility often demands a willingness to allow them to learn from their mistakes and be taught by pain and difficulty.

Do Your Best . . . and Let God Do the Rest

I laughed the other day when one of my friends confessed that at every parent-teacher conference she had ever attended for one of her children, the teacher had given her a "how-to" book on parenting. I sympathized with another friend's frustration over her son's academic lapse after she thought he had "turned the corner" and finally learned to be disciplined in his schoolwork. And I remembered our own struggles to teach our kids to control their tempers, to diligently practice the piano, to study for their tests *before* the very last minute, to take responsibility for keeping their rooms tidy, to stay in their chairs at the dinner table (they fall out of them with astonishing regularity), to use good manners . . . and the list goes on.

Here's the point: None of our children—even those who seem to be born with a measure of diligence or self-control—is perfect. And no matter how effectively we parent or how committed we are to disciplining, encouraging, and praying for our kids, we will never be "finished" with our jobs. Furthermore, we will make mistakes along the way. Parenting experts tell us to "be consistent," but I have yet to meet a mother who doesn't get tired, frustrated, or bewildered—especially when her best efforts seem to backfire.

But the good news is that God doesn't leave us to do the job on our own. When we pray for our children, we invite God to go to work in their lives. And, as Philippians 1:6 asserts, "he who began a good work in you will carry it on to completion until the day of Christ Jesus." I can't think of a more encouraging verse for frustrated or weary mothers as we pray for our kids and entrust them to God's care!

This very verse, in fact, was one I prayed for Hillary all last year. And as he so often does, God proved faithful to his promises. Once, after we had spent several weeks praying specifically for Hillary to exercise diligence and responsibility in her schoolwork, her report card came home with excellent marks. What's more, her teacher (who had no idea what we were praying for) had written a one-sentence note: "Hillary has worked so diligently and has shown great responsibility in learning and completing assignments." Of all the things the teacher *could* have commented on, she pointed to Hillary's diligence and responsibility! In addition to reinforcing our conviction that God hears our prayers, the teacher's remarks gave Hillary some tangible evidence of her heavenly Father's faithfulness and love—attributes she can depend on as she grows.

Prayer Principle _____

> When you pray for God to work in your children's lives, you can trust his promise to finish the job.

Poised for Prayer

Lest you think that stories of good grades and diligent work habits are the norm in our family, I'll swallow my pride and let you in on the truth: For every answer to prayer we experience, another challenge (or another child) is always waiting in the wings.

As I write this, for example, we are pouring on the prayer for Robbie who, as he approaches his fourth birthday, is in dire need of a dose of self-control.

The other day I overheard him calling one of his friends a name. I hustled to the scene of the crime, ready to launch into my best "ugly talk" sermonette. But what came out of my mouth wasn't a lecture. It was a prayer verse, plain and simple, taken from Proverbs 9:10: "Cause Robbie to fear you, Lord," I blurted out, "because that is the beginning of wisdom. Cause him to know you, and to have understanding."

I hadn't planned to say this; in fact, I couldn't have quoted Proverbs 9:10 had you asked me to. But no sooner were the words out of my mouth than Robbie turned to his friend and apologized for his unkind words. The two of them played happily for the rest of the day—and I learned a valuable lesson: As parents, we need to equip our minds and our hearts with Scripture so that we will be prepared to pray with wisdom and power in any situation.

Think about it: When our kids misbehave or struggle with a problem, there won't always be a Bible handy—and even if we could get our hands on one, how many of us would know where to look for an appropriate verse to pray? Even if you have never memorized Scripture before, or if you have a history of failed attempts to "lock in" any passages, try again—and ask God to help you. Start with just two or three "all-purpose" verses. Then, when you've gotten those down, build your "prayer bank" by adding Scriptures as you are able. The more you deposit, the more quickly and effectively you can make a withdrawal when the prayer needs arise.

A few of my favorite prayer verses include Ephesians 4:29 ("Do not let any unwholesome talk come out of your mouths, but only what is helpful for building others up according to their needs, that it may benefit those who listen"); Psalm 91:11 ("For he will command his angels concerning you to guard you in all your ways"); and Philippians 1:10 (that my children "may be able to discern what is best and may be pure and blameless until the day of Christ"). You might want to choose other verses that "fit" *your* kids better. Whatever verses you choose, take the time to learn them by heart. Then, when the prayer needs arise, you will be ready to approach God on your children's behalf.

Prayers You Can Use

Heavenly Father...

Thank you for disciplining _____, and for preparing him to share in your holiness. Use this discipline—however painful—to train him and produce a harvest of righteousness and peace in his life. (Hebrews 12:10–11)

❧

Help _____ to be self-controlled and pure, to be busy at home, to be kind, and to be subject to her husband, so that no one will malign the word of God. (Titus 2:5)

~

Help _____ to be self-controlled. Let him show integrity, seriousness, and soundness of speech that cannot be condemned, so that those who oppose the gospel may be ashamed because they have nothing bad to say about him. (Titus 2:6–8)

~

Set a guard over _____'s mouth, O Lord; keep watch over her lips. Don't let her heart be drawn to what is evil or allow her to take part in wicked deeds. (Psalm 141:3–4)

~

May _____'s sin find him out, so that he will be drawn back to you, Lord, for forgiveness and your gracious blessing of a new beginning. (Numbers 32:23)

~

Cause _____ to make every effort to add to her faith goodness; and to goodness, knowledge; and to knowledge, self-control; and to self-control, perseverance; and to perseverance, godliness; and to godliness, brotherly kindness; and to brotherly kindness, love. Let _____ possess these qualities in increasing measure, so that she will be effective and productive in her knowledge of our Lord Jesus Christ. (2 Peter 1:5–8)

∾

*M*ake _____ self-controlled and alert. His enemy the devil prowls around like a roaring lion looking for someone to devour. Help him to resist him and stand firm in the faith. *(1 Peter 5:8–9)*

∾

*P*repare _____'s mind for action. Let her be self-controlled, with her hope set fully on the grace to be given her when Jesus Christ is revealed. *(1 Peter 1:13)*

∾

*L*et _____ be diligent, O Lord, and satisfy all his desires. *(Proverbs 13:4)*

∾

*W*hatever _____ does, may she work at it with all her heart, as working for you, Lord, not for people. *(Colossians 3:23)*

∾

*D*o not give _____ a spirit of timidity, but a spirit of power, of love, and of self-discipline. *(2 Timothy 1:7)*

Part Three

Praying for Your Child's Safety

CHAPTER NINE

PRAYING FOR PHYSICAL HEALTH AND SAFETY

I will lie down and sleep in peace,
   for you alone, O LORD,
   make me dwell in safety.

—Psalm 4:8

BEFORE OUR DAUGHTER, VIRGINIA, WAS BORN, A ROUTINE ULTRA-sound revealed a cyst on her brain. Six weeks and countless prayers later, it had miraculously disappeared—but the scare turned out to be a portent of things to come. By the time Virginia reached her third birthday, she had piled up enough lumps, bumps, and bruises to fill the better part of a medical school textbook. She had lost a fingernail in the hinge of our bathroom door; split her chin open so badly that we had to get a plastic surgeon to meet us in the emergency room; tumbled down a flight of steps; and suffered so many black eyes and bloody lips that we gave up trying to get a "good" photograph of her, settling for "realistic" snapshots instead.

Finally, when Virginia *ate* part of a glass thermometer (we never did find the mercury; "poison control" assured us that the newer models were not toxic), I realized that something had to be done. She was tough—grinding the glass in her teeth didn't seem to faze her—but I wondered how long her luck would hold out. She was only four years old: What would become of her during her teenage years?

"God!" I found myself crying out, *"Aren't you paying attention? What happened to the 'hedge of protection' and the 'guardian angels' I asked you to provide for our children?"*

Almost immediately I sensed God's answer. "I *am* protecting Virginia," he spoke to my heart. "In fact, I've had to put some of my best angels on the job, just to keep her alive!"

It sounds funny now, but at the time this message was exactly what I needed to hear. As I realized that God really did care about Virginia's welfare—and that even when I could not watch or protect her, his angels were on duty—my complaints and accusations gave way to prayers of gratitude.

The reality of angelic ministry took on added significance in our lives last year. Each December I ask the Lord to give me a verse to pray for our children during the coming year, and last year he gave me Psalm 91:11 for Virginia: "For he will command his angels concerning you to guard you in all your ways." I have prayed this verse for Virginia again and again, and God has proved incredibly faithful to his promise. Not only has Virginia avoided any disfiguring injuries since I started specifically praying for her protection, but she has never even been sick—not even with a winter cold!

I realize that my Psalm 91:11 prayer is not some magical health-and-safety "guarantee," and I know that God—for reasons I probably will not fully understand—may one day allow Virginia to suffer physically, but when I stop to consider all the times in the past year that she *could* have been hurt—jumping on the trampoline, learning to ride a bicycle, and just generally being a kid—I cannot help but believe that God is doing a mighty work in answer to a mother's heartfelt prayer, and that his angels really are on their toes.

Prayer Principle _____

> Prayers for your children's safety may be rooted in the certainty that God loves them, and that the Lord is always alert and on the job.

_____ ∿

"Lord, Why Did This Happen?"

I know I'm not the only mother who has ever questioned God's tactics. Even my "spiritual giant" friend, Susan, found herself wondering what was up when her son Michael started suffering from violent stomach pains. Their pediatrician had dismissed the problem as nothing more than a flu bug, but when the symptoms persisted and Susan began noticing blood in the little boy's urine, she and her husband, Randy, decided to consult a specialist. A battery of tests confirmed their worst fears: Just three-and-a-half years old, Michael had something called Berger's disease—an illness that, according to the doctors, was almost always fatal.

Susan was overcome with sadness and confusion. Why did this have to happen to her precious boy? Could it have been prevented? Had she given him too much milk as a baby, or omitted something critical from his diet? Was God trying to punish her for some unconfessed sin?

Hurling accusations at herself and at God, Susan picked up her Bible and turned to John 9, the passage she was scheduled to read for her Bible study. In it, Jesus encountered a man who had been blind from birth. "Rabbi," his disciples asked, "who sinned, this man or his parents, that he was born blind?"

Susan's heart leaped into her throat as she read Jesus' answer: "Neither this man nor his parents sinned, but this happened so that the work of God might be displayed in his life."

This happened so that the work of God might be displayed in his life. Reading those words, Susan felt God's peace welling up inside her, along with the sudden realization that he was in control. For the first time since Michael's ordeal had begun months earlier, Susan found herself willing and able to set aside her own desires—namely, that her son would be healed—and begin to pray what she called "bigger picture" prayers. She prayed for the young girl in the hospital bed next to Michael's, and the impact that their family's faith might have on the girl and on her family. She prayed for the doctors and the hospital staff. She prayed for Michael to see God's providence and blessing, even in the midst of his fear and pain. And most of all, she prayed that God would be glorified.

"The idea that Michael's illness was an opportunity for God to work really set me free," Susan later told me. "I was able to take my eyes off of our problems and focus on God and his purposes." And God's purposes, as it turned out, included a welcome surprise: Michael's "illness" ultimately revealed itself as nothing more than a kidney stone—incredibly painful, but easily removed, and not at all life-threatening!

Prayer Principle _____

When you pray for your children's health and safety, it helps to keep your eyes fixed on Jesus—not on the circumstances.

From Tragedy to Triumph

You would be hard-pressed to find a mother who would not understand or sympathize with Susan's initial fear and confusion. As anyone who has ever momentarily "lost" a child on a crowded beach or in the racks of a department store can tell you, it doesn't take much to send our maternal instincts into overdrive. And in an age when threats to our kids' safety seem to lurk around every corner, our fears—whether justifiable or not—can easily ignite our imagination.

Our Moms In Touch group routinely prays for our children's safety, both at school and as they go to and from the school grounds. Last year, a first grader was struck by a car as he crossed the street to board his waiting school bus. All of us knew the boy and his family, and we spent the day crying out to the Lord on his behalf and waiting for news of his condition. Later that day, when we learned he had died, our grief—as individuals and as an entire community—was immeasurable.

"Why, Lord?" my heart cried. *"This boy was one we had prayed for by name—how could you have let him die? Wasn't his name engraved on the palms of your hands?"*[1]

I do not know why God allowed this precious child to die. As I prayed for his family, though, the Lord reminded me of Isaiah 55:8–9, the passage he gave me years ago when two of my closest friends were killed in an airplane crash: "'For my thoughts are not your thoughts, neither are your ways my ways,' declares the LORD. 'As the heavens are higher than the earth, so are my ways higher than your ways and my thoughts than your thoughts.'"

More recently, I have found comfort in how King David handled his own son's death. As 2 Samuel 12:15–23 tells it, David was a basket case during the boy's illness, refusing to eat or even to get up from the ground. But when the child died, David's response surprised everyone. He got up, washed, changed his clothes, and went to worship the Lord. When his servants asked about his emotional turnaround, David explained that while his son was still alive, he fasted and wept in hopes that God would let the child live. "But now that he is dead," he said, "why should I fast? Can I bring him back again? I will go to him, but he will not return to me."[2]

I will go to him. In this simple phrase David revealed his understanding of eternity. For Christians, death is never the end. And for parents who lose a child here on earth, I cannot think of a more encouraging vision than that of a heavenly reunion with their beloved. Our earthly pain and grief may seem endless, but as King David must have known, they are nothing compared to the boundless joy of life on "the other side."

And, at the risk of sounding like a Pollyanna, I believe that those who trust in God's goodness can experience a measure of joy on *this* side of heaven as well. Fern Nichols, founder and president of Moms In Touch International, notes that, despite Satan's attempts to discourage and defeat us, "God can take tragedy and turn it into triumph. He routinely does this for those who love him."[3]

Perhaps nowhere was this transformation more evident than at Columbine High School, where twelve teenagers and one teacher were killed by two student gunmen on April 20, 1999. Despite their unfathomable grief, local pastors, teachers, students, and even parents of slain students have seen God's hand in the spiritual revival that has made Columbine a national touchpoint. Alisa Long, leader of Columbine's Moms In Touch group, wrote the following:

> We had prayed that Columbine would be a light to the rest of the world. God answered our prayers in greater ways than we could have imagined. In my whole lifetime, I have never seen God working so visibly....
>
> People indifferent to God, people wondering who God is, people who had put Him aside are thinking about Him again. Even hardened students said, "I saw God at Columbine." Our limited view has exploded as we have watched the Lord in action and know "that was God."
>
> ... What Satan meant for destruction, God has restored a hundredfold. Instead of losing children at that school, the Lord has increased his flock.
>
> My message to moms is keep praying. He is there. He won't forget you.[4]

Prayer Principle _____

> You can always pray with confidence, knowing that
> what Satan means for harm, God uses for good—even
> when human eyes can't see any possible way to
> turn tragedy into triumph.

_____ ∽

Poised for Prayer

As I pray for my kids' health and safety, events like the Columbine shootings are never very far from my mind. Even so, I can pray for their protection with confidence, knowing that, as the Columbine mom put it, "God is there, and he won't forget us."

How can I be so confident? First, because God promised that he *will* hear me when he said, "Call to me and I will answer you."[5] Not only that, but I know that when I turn God's promises into prayers for my children, the words carry power. Isaiah 55:11 says that God's word will not return empty, but will accomplish his desires and purposes. These purposes might not always be the ones I have in mind, but because I know that God sees "the big picture," I can rest assured that his perspective is the right one.

Also, I know that God loves my children and that he truly wants the best for them. Romans 8:28 says, "And we know that in all things God works for the good of those who love him, who have been called according to his purpose." This doesn't mean we won't face adversity—in fact, the Bible pretty much guarantees that we will. (See, for example, Matthew 13:21; John 15:20; 2 Corinthians 4:8–9; and 2 Corinthians 12:10.) But when God allows my children to suffer, I know he will use the experience to build their faith, their patience, and their strength.

Most of all, my confidence in praying for my kids' safety and protection is rooted in the fact that God sent his only Son to suffer and die on the cross. Never having experienced the loss of a child, I can only imagine how Christ's bitter agony must have pierced the Father's heart. For God to allow that to happen, it is inconceivable to me that nearly two thousand years later he would turn around and hand Satan the ultimate victory in my children's lives. To do so would deny his unlimited power. It would mock his undying love. And it would render Christ's death meaningless.

In other words, it would be unthinkable.

Prayers You Can Use

Heavenly Father...

I pray that _____ will enjoy good health and that all will go well with him. (3 John 2)

❧

*D*on't let _____ be wise in her own eyes; rather, cause her to fear you and shun evil. You have promised that this will bring health to her body and nourishment to her bones. (Proverbs 3:7–8)

∾

*W*hen _____ is set upon by bullies or assaulted by other wickedness, please help him and deliver him. Deliver him from the wicked and save him, because he takes refuge in you. (Psalm 37:40)

∾

*L*et _____ lie down and sleep in peace. (Psalm 4:8)— (God must have had mothers of newborns and sick children in mind when he gave us this verse!)

∾

*T*hank you that you have redeemed _____ and called her by name; she is yours. When she passes through the waters (trials, temptations, peer pressure, suffering, and the like), be with her. When she passes through the rivers, do not let them sweep over her. When she walks through the fire, do not let her be burned. (Isaiah 43:1–2)

∾

*L*et _____ take refuge in you and be glad; let him ever sing for joy. Spread your protection over _____ that he may rejoice in you. (Psalm 5:11)

❧

*L*ord, you are faithful. Please strengthen and protect
_____ from the evil one. (2 Thessalonians 3:3)

❧

*G*ive _____ victory and be her shield. Guard her course
and protect her way. (Proverbs 2:7–8)

❧

*T*hank you that Jesus bore our sins in his body on the tree,
and that by his wounds _____ is healed. (1 Peter 2:24)

❧

*L*et _____ dwell in the shelter of the Most High and rest
in the shadow of the Almighty. Be his refuge, his fortress,
his covering, his shield. Do not let him fear the terror of the
night, nor any type of plague or sickness. Do not let any
harm or disaster come near _____. Command your
angels to guard him in all his ways and keep him from hurting himself. When he calls on you, answer him. Be with him
in trouble; deliver him and honor him. Satisfy _____ with
long life and show him your salvation. (Psalm 91)

CHAPTER TEN

PRAYING FOR SPIRITUAL PROTECTION

And lead us not into temptation,
but deliver us from the evil one.

—Matthew 6:13

I REMEMBER THE DREAM AS THOUGH IT HAPPENED YESTERDAY. I heard the doorbell ring, and when I opened the door, six or seven children were crowded on our front stoop. They were a seedy-looking bunch, jostling one another for space on our small porch. I started to greet them, but then I noticed that they weren't looking at me. They were trying to peer around me into our front hall.

"Come with us!" they whispered, still craning their necks and elbowing one another. "Come with us!"

I knew instinctively that these youngsters—whose faces I could not see clearly—were beckoning to my children. I had no idea why they wanted our kids to come out or what they wanted to do, only that it was something of ugly or evil intent, something that Robbie and I would not want our kids to participate in, or even to know about.

"Come with us!"

As the whispers grew louder and more insistent, I stood my ground, blocking the view into our home. I was not angry—just determined. "You cannot do this," I said. "The children in this house have been prayed for since even before they were born—and you have no authority here!"

With that, the little crowd vanished, leaving my doorstep deserted.

The dream left a strong impression on my mind, and a few days later I shared this story with my prayer group. "I think," I said, "that the Lord wants to encourage us that our prayers really do make a difference, and to remind us that when we pray for our children, we can't do it with a routine or half-hearted mentality. We need to pray for our kids with the same tenacity and determination we would exercise if we were trying to fend off a wild dog or some other visible threat."

Asking God to protect our children may be a mother's most oft-repeated prayer. But more often than not, our prayers center around *physical* protection, ignoring the invisible—but incredibly potent—dangers in the *spiritual* realm. And these unseen threats are very real. As Ephesians 6:12 says, "For our struggle is not against flesh and blood, but against the rulers, against the authorities, against the powers of this dark world and against the spiritual forces of evil in the heavenly realms."

To ignore Satan or to deny that he and his fellow demons are at work today is to play right into their hands. As C. S. Lewis put it, "There are two equal and opposite errors into which our race can fall about the devils. One is to disbelieve in their existence. The other is to believe, and to feel an excessive and unhealthy interest in them. They themselves are equally pleased by both errors, and hail a materialist or a magician with the same delight."[1]

What do these "powers of this dark world" look like today? At the risk of sounding paranoid, Satan's mark can be found just about anywhere, from books, music, and movies to cults and false religions. He can creep into our lives when other things or interests—sports, possessions, careers, accomplishments, and the like—begin to take the place of God. His influence may appear in a blatant form (such as witchcraft) or hide behind more subtle deceptions (like the "religion" of secular humanism). It's not always easy to tell what's what. Satan, the Bible says, "masquerades as an angel of light" and his servants "masquerade as servants of righteousness."[2]

But the purpose of this chapter is not to point fingers or to make you nervous about the devil and his minions, but simply to remind you that they do exist—and to encourage you to pray for your children's protection. Remember: For those who belong to God, there is no reason to fear, since, as 1 John 4:4 reminds us, "the one [that is, Christ Jesus] who is in you is greater than the one who is in the world."

Prayer Principle _____

You can pray for your children's spiritual protection with joy, faith, and assurance, knowing that Christ Jesus is greater than any of the dark forces that inhabit their world.

We Are Weak, but He Is Strong

Nathan looked forward to going to Bosnia with his father, Dennis. Not only would the mission trip afford Nathan and others from his church a chance to teach English to the Bosnians (and thereby offer hope for their economic future), but the Americans were also planning to share the gospel with people who had never heard it before. Nathan was especially excited about his own particular role on the mission team: An outstanding athlete, he was to build relationships with the Bosnian children through basketball camps designed to get kids off the streets and introduce them to Jesus.

In preparation for the trip, Nathan and his family had memorized Psalm 121, in which God promises to "not let your foot slip" and to "keep you from all harm." At age sixteen, Nathan felt virtually invincible—and was therefore stunned when, just before he was scheduled to leave on the Bosnia trip, he learned that a stubborn mass on his collarbone might be cancer. Several tests ultimately revealed the problem to be nothing more than muscle growth, but the temporary scare replaced his "invincible" feeling with one of dependence on God.

This dependence proved vital when Nathan arrived in Bosnia—and his luggage didn't. How was he supposed to run a basketball camp without any gear? To make matters worse, almost as soon as they got the camp up and running, Nathan was sidelined again, this time with a knee injury—suffered on the very day he was scheduled to share his Christian testimony with the Bosnians.

There was little question that Nathan was under some kind of spiritual attack, but when his mother, Monica, heard what had happened, her trust in God's provision and protection did not waver. "You have promised not to let his foot slip or stumble," she reminded God, quoting from Psalm 121. "You have also promised to keep him from all harm. I don't know what you are doing in Nathan's life, Lord, but I praise you that your purposes are greater than ours."

As things turned out, Nathan never got to play basketball the way he had envisioned he would. Instead, he found himself indebted to the Bosnians, and he was humbled by their attitude of gratefulness and generosity as they cared for him in the aftermath of his injury. Satan had tried to thwart Nathan's testimony, but—once again—God used the circumstances to advance the gospel, both in Nathan's life and in the lives of the Bosnian children. Nathan learned humility and the art of receiving love, while the experience built relationships and opened discussions with his Bosnian hosts that might never have been possible on the basketball court. God, Nathan later reflected, got his attention—and proved that his power really is made perfect in weakness.[3]

Prayer Principle _____

When God allows your children to stumble or slip, he gives you the opportunity to pray for his power to manifest itself in their lives and his strength to be made perfect in their weakness.

Protection in God's Presence

Allison's teenage son, Eric, attended a private school where weekly chapel services served as a shadowy reminder of the school's religious origins. Most of the chapel speakers espoused the Christian faith, but from time to time school administrators invited representatives of other world religions to address the student body—both to teach the students about other faiths and to underscore the school's emphasis on diversity.

"Mom," Eric said one day, "tomorrow a Hindu man is going to speak at chapel. Some of the guys aren't too happy about it, but there's nothing we can do."

Allison knew that the "guys" Eric was referring to were in his closest circle of friends, almost all of whom were believers in Jesus Christ. "Have you prayed about it?" Allison asked.

"No," Eric admitted. "Not really. Would you pray, Mom?"

Allison and Eric prayed according to Philippians 4:7, that the peace of God, which transcends all understanding, would guard the hearts and minds of every student in the chapel service.

The next day Eric burst through their kitchen door, his face flushed with excitement. "Mom!" he cried. "You'll never guess what happened! Today, when the Hindu guy started to speak, almost everyone fell asleep! I looked around, and I couldn't believe it—the guys and I were praying during the service, and I guess God must have heard us. Nobody was listening to the speaker; the whole audience seemed to be either sleeping or praying!"

When I heard this story, it reminded me of when Hannah sent her son, Samuel, to live with Eli, the temple priest.[4] Just as Allison could not accompany her son to school, so Hannah could not stay with Samuel (who was only a young boy) when she took him to the temple. To say that the temple atmosphere was not conducive to holy living and spiritual growth might be an understatement; Eli's own sons were wicked men who routinely stole sacrificial meats and slept with the women who served outside the temple.

Yet Hannah never faltered in her determination to give her son to the Lord. Instead of worrying about him, she prayed, rejoicing in what God had done for her and trusting him to guard the feet of his saints and silence the wicked. This prayer, recorded in 1 Samuel 2:1–10, serves as a wonderful model for contemporary mothers to follow.

We can't go everywhere with our kids, but, as Hannah undoubtedly knew, our prayers can. And what's even more comforting is the fact that even though we cannot always be by our child's side, *God can*. Hannah gave her son to God, and Samuel "grew up in the presence of the LORD."[5]

Given the threats and dangers our children face today—many of which we can't even see—knowing that God is with them makes all the difference. He will be with them everywhere they go, whether it's across the world to a foreign country or across the street to a friend's house.

Prayer Principle _____

Praying that your children will "grow up in the presence of the LORD" is an invaluable way to pray for their protection—both now and in the years ahead.

Poised for Prayer

When it comes to praying for spiritual protection, Scripture is full of battle imagery and vivid descriptions of the "weapons" Christians are supposed to use when we wage war against the evil one. The best way I've found to get my kids outfitted for the battles they will face is to prayerfully clothe them in the "armor of God," as described in Ephesians 6:10–18.

First, I pray that they will be strong in the Lord rather than relying on their own strength of mind or will. Then, I put the armor on them, piece by piece: The belt of truth, the breastplate of righteousness, feet that are ready to carry the gospel, the shield of faith (handy for extinguishing Satan's flaming arrows), the helmet of salvation, and the sword of the Spirit, which is God's word. Finally, I ask God to keep them alert and enable them to pray effectively on all occasions.

If your children are very young and still need help getting dressed in the morning, you can turn this daily ritual into a powerful prayer session as you wrap them in their garments, both physical and spiritual. If they are older, you can pray that they will wear God's armor as you fold their laundry, shop for their clothes, or pack their suitcases for summer camp. Find a word or task association that works well for you, and as you pray for your children, remember the promise in Psalm 34:7: "The angel of the LORD encamps around those who fear him, and he delivers them."

❧ Prayers You Can Use ❧

Heavenly Father...

Keep _____ from all harm. Watch over his life; watch over his coming and going, both now and forevermore. (Psalm 121:7–8)

❧

Lead _____ not into temptation, but deliver her from the evil one. (Matthew 6:13)

❧

Put a hedge of protection and blessing around _____ and everything he has. (Job 1:10)

❧

Give _____ the weapons she needs to demolish strongholds, arguments, and every pretension that sets itself up against the knowledge of you, Lord. Help _____ to take captive every thought she has to make it obedient to Christ. (2 Corinthians 10:4–5)

❧

*H*elp _____ to submit to you, O God, and to resist the devil. Make the devil flee from _____ as he draws near to you. (James 4:7–8)

∽

*D*o not remove _____ from the pressures and trials of this world, but protect her from the evil one. Remind her that she belongs to you, not to the world. (John 17:14–15)

∽

*K*eep _____ from the snares the enemy has laid for him, from the traps set by evildoers. Let the wicked fall into their own nets, while he passes by in safety. (Psalm 141:9–10)

∽

*S*how _____ how to put off her old self, which is being corrupted by its deceitful desires, and make her new in the attitude of her mind. Cause her to put off falsehood and speak truthfully, and to refrain from sin when she is angry. Above all, do not let _____ do anything that would give the devil a foothold in her life. (Ephesians 4:22–27)

∽

*C*lothe _____ with your full armor so that he can take his stand against the devil's schemes. Help him to stand firm, with the belt of truth buckled around his waist and the breastplate of righteousness in place. Fit his feet with the *readiness that comes from the gospel of peace. Give _____ the shield of faith, with which he can extinguish all the flaming arrows of the evil one. Place the helmet of salvation on his head and the sword of the Spirit, which is your word, in his hands. Finally, teach him to pray, and to be alert. (Ephesians 6:11–18)*

∾

Keep men of perverse heart far from _____, and let her have nothing to do with evil. (Psalm 101:4)

∾

Do not let anyone lead _____ astray. Cause him to do what is righteous rather than what is sinful. Thank you for sending your Son to destroy the devil's work. (1 John 3:7–8)

CHAPTER ELEVEN

PRAYING FOR YOUR CHILD'S EMOTIONAL WELL-BEING

I praise you because I am fearfully and wonderfully made;
    your works are wonderful,
    I know that full well.

—Psalm 139:14

SEVERAL YEARS AGO MY FRIEND, LUCY, WAS ASKED TO SHARE HER testimony at a women's Bible study meeting. She nearly refused, on the grounds that she didn't have much of a story to tell—at least not one she thought would interest anyone. No sordid past, no period of teenage rebellion, no intellectual atheism or bouts with spiritual doubt. Yet when she finally agreed to speak, her words served as a potent witness to the power of love.

Lucy explained that her parents had become Christians when she was a young girl, and their newfound awareness of God's love spilled over into their parenting techniques. Rarely did they miss an opportunity to remind Lucy and her siblings

131

that they belonged to the Lord and had been created in God's image.[1] Sometimes the lessons were consciously administered, such as when Lucy's parents encouraged their children to memorize Bible verses that pointed to God's love. At other times, the message of love and acceptance seemed almost offhand: "Lucy," they would simply say, "we think you are wonderful."

It's been more than ten years since I heard Lucy speak, but I often remember her when I think about how many other girls grow up seeking love and acceptance through sexual relationships or attaching self-worth to their outward appearance. Likewise, when I hear about boys becoming bullies in their search for acceptance and respect, or when I read about schoolyard murders and other crimes committed by "loners," "misfits," or "outcasts," I can't help but wonder if things would be different had these children grown up in a home like Lucy's.

I am not a psychologist, and I won't pretend to understand why these things happen. Nevertheless, I am firmly convinced that a child's sense of self-worth, his feelings of love and acceptance, and his overall emotional well-being—as well as how he thinks and behaves—have more to do with his identity in Christ than anything else. Without the knowledge that he is precious in God's sight—not because of anything he has *done*, but simply because he *belongs* to the Lord—true emotional health becomes virtually impossible to attain.

Put another way, not every child can make straight As, become captain of his football team, or win the starring role in the school play. But every child can know what Lucy knew: that she is fearfully and wonderfully made, that God valued her enough to send his Son to die on her behalf, and that nothing—absolutely nothing—can separate her from God's love.[2]

Prayer Principle _____

Asking God to fill your children with the knowledge that they are "fearfully and wonderfully made," that they belong to God, and that they are precious in his sight can lay the groundwork for a lifetime of emotional security and health.

_____

The Forgiveness Factor

As soon as her daughter, Megan, arrived home from school, Kim knew something was wrong. Moments later, the story spilled out: A boy in Megan's class had carelessly remarked on her weight, saying she was fat.

"Mom," Megan said softly, "I know I'm bigger than the other girls in my class. But no one has ever *said* anything about it before."

Megan's words pierced Kim's heart. The daughter of deaf parents, she knew what it was like to be misunderstood and even mocked by her peers. "Oh, honey," she soothed, "it's what's on the inside that counts, not what you look like. You are a beautiful girl."

Later that evening, when Megan's father, Doug, heard what had happened, he reaffirmed Kim's words. "You are lovely to us—inside and out. And you are beautiful to God, too," he said. "But you need to forgive that boy for what he said, just as God forgives us when we do wrong things. You can't allow anger or bitterness or hurt feelings to steal your joy."

Megan and her parents prayed, and she chose to forgive her classmate for his offense. Two days later, a small miracle occurred: The boy called to ask for her address so he could invite her to a party! Megan accepted gladly, and their friendship (along with her joy) was fully restored.

How wise Megan's father was in refusing to let bitterness gain a foothold in his daughter's life. I suspect he knew that forgiveness is a choice, and that it is not dependent on how we *feel* (wounded or angry) but on what we *know* (that just as God forgives us, so he commands us to extend mercy to others).[3] I'll never forget trying to convince our young neighbor, Tee, to forgive Annesley after she had hit him with a toy. "Do you think you can forgive her?" I asked.

"Yes," Tee whimpered, "but it *still* hurts!"

Forgiveness doesn't always make a hurt go away, and it never makes what someone said or did okay. But it sets us free from the bondage of bitterness and paves the way for contentment, peace, and joy. As we pray for our children, let's pray that they will love their enemies, do good to those who hate them, bless those who curse them, and pray for those who mistreat them.[4] Let's ask God to give them a spirit of forgiveness, and keep them ever mindful of the Golden Rule: "Do to others as you would have them do to you."[5]

Prayer Principle _____

> Praying for your child to have a forgiving spirit is a tool you can use to keep bitterness and anger from gaining a foothold in her life.

The Secret to Contentment and Joy

While I was writing this book, our family moved from Winston-Salem, North Carolina, to San Diego, California. Not knowing anyone in the San Diego area, and with virtually all of our extended family members hunkered down on the East Coast, Robbie and I wondered how our children would respond when we told them we were moving. Visions of Hillary sobbing over our last move—from Atlanta to Winston-Salem—were still fresh in our minds. At that time she had been just six years old; how would she react to another move at age ten, when peer relationships were a much more significant part of her life? All of our kids, for that matter, were old enough to know what was involved in a move; how would any of them respond?

When we told the children about the move, God gave me an interesting picture to share with them. "Imagine it's Christmas morning," I said, "and the gifts under the tree are from God. You've already opened some of them. The first one was Atlanta—remember how much we loved living there?"

The kids all nodded; we've kept in close touch with many of our friends in Atlanta, and our family cherishes the memory of the time we spent in that city.

"The next present we opened," I continued, "was Winston-Salem. God has been so good to us here, giving us a home and a school and friends we love. It's hard to think about leaving this place, isn't it?"

Again the kids agreed. None of them had any desire to leave North Carolina.

"But guess what?" I said. "There's another present under the tree, and it's got each of our names written on it. Do we want to open it and see what else God wants to give us—or should we just keep playing with the gifts we've already opened?"

There was a second or two of silence as the kids thought about the question. Then, almost as one, they jumped to their feet. "Open it! Open it!" they cried. Knowing how much they loved the "presents" God had already given us, they were able to embrace the idea of another gift—another move—with eagerness and enthusiasm.

I won't pretend that leaving Winston-Salem was easy; it's never fun to say good-bye to the people you love. Nor can I say that the first few weeks in our new community were entirely tear-free. But because our children know (1) that God is good, (2) that he is in charge, and (3) that he loves us and wants what is best for each one of us, they have been able to experience contentment and joy—even in the face of a cross-country move.

Prayer Principle _____

> Praying for your children to trust in God's promises and depend on his love can turn their hearts into a dwelling place for genuine joy—even when things go wrong.

Poised for Prayer

Proverbs 27:19 says that "as water reflects a face, so a man's heart reflects the man." Think about your children, one by one.

What do their hearts look like? Are their lives marked by peace, joy, contentment, and security—or do they consistently wrestle with uncertainty, discouragement, depression, and fear?

Negative attitudes can be both habit-forming and physically dangerous—as Proverbs 14:30 puts it: "A heart at peace gives life to the body, but envy rots the bones." If you sense a need for some change (or if you simply want to ensure that negative tendencies don't become habits), start by working on your child's sense of self-worth. Fill her mind with the knowledge that she is precious to the God of all creation—and that she *belongs* to him. Read Psalm 139 aloud, and encourage your family to memorize selected verses—or better still, the entire thing. Pray these verses over your children as you drive them to school, as you think about them during the day, and as you tuck them into bed at night.

Next, read the book of Philippians. It's a short but powerful course on Christian joy, and it offers some great advice on how to ward off life's joy stealers: circumstances, people, things, and worry—the four thieves identified in Warren Wiersbe's commentary, *Be Joyful*.[6] If you really want to get serious about bringing joy into your home, get a copy of this book and start putting the Philippians' principles to work.

Finally, reaffirm your trust in God's promises. In John 15:10–11, Jesus says that if we obey him and remain in his love, his joy will remain in us and our joy will be complete. Joy isn't something the Lord reserves for upbeat, "bubbly" people. Rather, godly joy—the kind that comes from resting and remaining in God's love—is for everyone.

As you pray for your family, borrow a prayer from the psalmist: "Satisfy us in the morning with your unfailing love, that we may sing for joy and be glad *all our days*."[7]

❧ Prayers You Can Use ❧

Heavenly Father...

Cause _____ to love her enemies, to do good to those who hate her, to bless those who curse her, to pray for those who mistreat her. Help _____ do to others as she would have them do to her. (Luke 6:27–31)

❧

Let _____ be quick to confess sin, knowing that you are faithful and just, and that you will forgive him his sins and purify him from all unrighteousness. Don't let him get bogged down by his past mistakes; rather, remind him that he is a new creation in Christ, that the old has gone and the new has come! (1 John 1:9; 2 Corinthians 5:17)

❧

I pray that _____'s identity will be firmly rooted and established in Christ's love, and that _____ may have power, together with all the saints, to grasp how wide and long and high and deep is the love of Christ, and to know this love that surpasses knowledge—that she may be filled to the measure of all the fullness of God. (Ephesians 3:17–19)

❧

*L*et _____ be filled with the joy given by the Holy Spirit. Let _____ be joyful always, pray continually, and give thanks in all circumstances, for this is your will for him in Christ Jesus. *(1 Thessalonians 1:6; 5:16–18)*

∾

*D*o not let _____ be enslaved by her emotions. Christ has set her free, so let her stand firm, refusing to let herself be burdened again by a yoke of slavery. *(Galatians 5:1)*

∾

*L*et _____ grow as Jesus did, in wisdom and stature, and in favor with God and men. *(Luke 2:52)*

∾

*L*et the light of your face shine upon _____. Fill his heart with joy, and let him lie down and sleep in peace. *(Psalm 4:6–8)*

∾

*S*how _____ that she is fearfully and wonderfully made, and that your works are wonderful. Teach her that she is precious in your sight, and that you love her. *(Psalm 139:14; Isaiah 43:4)*

∾

*L*et _____ make every effort to win your praise, rather than seeking the approval of his peers. Show _____ that the fear of man is a snare, but he who trusts in you will be kept safe. (John 5:44; Proverbs 29:25)

❧

*B*estow on _____ all the goodness you have stored up for her because she fears you. When her feelings are hurt, be her shelter and her refuge, and keep her safe from the strife of unkind words. (Psalm 31:19–20)

❧

*W*hen _____ is confronted with grief, uncertainty, fear, or pressure, remind him of your promise in Isaiah 41:10: "Do not fear, for I am with you; do not be dismayed, for I am your God. I will strengthen you and help you; I will uphold you with my righteous right hand."

❧

*L*et _____ know that she belongs to you. (Romans 14:7–9)

CHAPTER TWELVE

PRAYING FOR KIDS IN CRISIS

> Fear not, for I have redeemed you;
>   I have summoned you by name; you are mine.
> When you pass through the waters,
>   I will be with you;
> and when you pass through the rivers,
>   they will not sweep over you.
> When you walk through the fire,
>   you will not be burned;
>   the flames will not set you ablaze.

—Isaiah 43:1–2

IN 2 KINGS 4:8–37, SCRIPTURE TELLS THE STORY OF A CHILDLESS couple who befriended Elisha and added a guest room to their house for the prophet to use whenever he would come to town. In return for their kindness, Elisha promised that the woman, a Shunammite, would have a son the following year. Despite her disbelief, things happened just as Elisha said they would. She gave birth to a beautiful little boy, her only son.

One day, though, the child complained of a headache. The woman held him on her lap for several hours and watched, helpless, as the life ebbed out of her little boy. When he died, she laid him on Elisha's bed and left the room, shutting the door behind her. She then called her husband and asked for a servant and a donkey, that she might "go to the man of God quickly and return."[1] No mention is made of her telling her husband what the problem was; she simply assured him that things were "all right" and then set out to find Elisha.

While the Shunammite woman was still some distance away, Elisha saw her and sent his servant to ask whether everything was okay. "Everything is all right," she repeated. But when she made it to Elisha and he finally realized what had happened, the prophet immediately dispatched his servant, telling him to run to the boy and lay Elisha's staff on the child's face.

But the Shunammite woman would have nothing to do with this plan. "As surely as the LORD lives and as you live," she told Elisha, "I will not leave you."[2] Faced with a mother's love and perseverance, Elisha got up and followed her home.

And it was a good thing he did. The servant, who had gone on ahead, could get no response out of the dead boy, even when he used Elisha's staff, as the prophet had told him to. When Elisha arrived, he went into the room, shut the door, and started to pray, stretching himself out on the boy's little body. Within moments, the child returned to life. Elisha summoned the woman, who came into the room, saw what had happened, bowed at Elisha's feet—and then took her son and left the room.

As a mother, I find this story nothing short of incredible. I can pretty much guarantee you that if one of my children were to die in my lap, my first response would *not* be to say that everything was "all right." But what an inspiring lesson the Shunammite woman offers! When confronted with a devastating situation, her response revealed a deep and abiding trust in God.

In *Experiencing God*, authors Henry Blackaby and Claude King note that the word *crisis* comes from a word that means "decision." How we live our lives, they say, is a testimony to what we believe about God. When we face a "crisis of belief"—a turning point where we must make a decision—how we respond (that is, what we do next) reveals what we really believe about God.[3]

The Shunammite woman had no assurance that Elisha could restore her son to life. In fact, if you read her actual words in the Bible, it appears that she was looking to Elisha more for an explanation than for a miracle. But, regardless of her intentions, one fact is clear: In a crisis situation, this mother refused to let fear or anger separate her from God's love.

Prayer Principle

When your child is in a crisis situation, how you pray and what you do reveals what you really believe about God.

Putting Your Child's Life in God's Hands

Jim Cymbala and his wife, Carol, would understand the anguish the Shunammite woman must have faced as she watched her son's life slip away. As the pastor of the 6,000-plus-member multicultural Brooklyn Tabernacle, Jim has seen God's life-changing power at work in countless situations, many of which could easily be described as "well beyond the crisis stage." But for all of Jim's teaching on faith and prayer, he was not prepared to deal with the change he saw in his teenage daughter, Chrissy, when she began to slip away—both from God and from their family.

You can read their remarkable story in Jim's book, *Fresh Wind, Fresh Fire*. As Chrissy's situation worsened, Jim writes, "I begged, I pleaded, I scolded, I argued, I tried to control her with money." He also prayed, but admits that he couldn't help wanting to take matters into his own hands. "I was still," he says, "the point guard wanting to grab the basketball, push it down the floor, make something happen, press through any hole in the defense I could find. But the more I pressed, the worse Chrissy got."[4]

Eventually, Jim realized his mistake. By relying on his own efforts, cleverness, and energy, he was playing right into Satan's hands. "The truth of the matter," Jim points out, "is that the devil is not terribly frightened of our human efforts and credentials. But he knows his kingdom will be damaged when we lift up our hearts to God."[5]

And so Jim and Carol began to really pray, believing God's promise in Jeremiah 33:3: "Call to me and I will answer you and tell you great and unsearchable things you do not know." They found encouragement and confidence in King David's assertion in Psalm 4:3: "Know that the LORD has set apart the godly for himself; the LORD will hear when I call to him." They quit maneuvering, cajoling, and crying, and they got serious about calling on God—and an incredible thing happened. I won't spoil their story by giving away the details; I'd rather you read the firsthand account in Jim's book. Suffice it to say, though, that the Lord moved in answer to their prayers, and Jim and Carol realized an amazing truth: God cannot resist those who humbly and honestly admit how desperately they need him.[6]

Prayer Principle _____

> When prayer is your only option, you are in an
> excellent position to see God move.

Thomas's Story: God's Blessings in Adversity

In a nation where every day sees 13 kids commit suicide, 1,000 become mothers, 130,000 bring guns to school, and 500 begin using drugs, stories like that of the Cymbalas are more common than any parent would like to imagine.[7] But the term *crisis* is not confined to teenagers and the issues they face. A crisis can erupt in the wake of any number of events: the death of a grandparent, a move to a new city or to a different school system, a falling-out among peers, or the discovery of a physical illness or a disability.

Our friends, Nancy and Rich, have three sons, spanning the ages of five through twelve. Each of the boys is bright, talented, and outgoing, but there is something irresistible about their youngest son, Thomas. He reminds me of a puppy dog or a teddy bear—you just can't help wanting to scoop him up in your arms. Once I even paid him to let me hold him for awhile. (He wanted twenty bucks but settled for a quarter.) And when Thomas has something to say—which is often— adults almost always crouch down to his level to listen.

I met Thomas when he was two years old. He wore glasses then, as he still does, not because he is nearsighted or farsighted, but to protect his eyes against rocks, sticks, or other projectiles little boys love to launch. Thomas sees perfectly out of one eye, but he is completely blind in the other, the result of an inoperable tumor that has entwined itself around his optic nerve.

The tumor is a manifestation of an even more serious problem. Thomas has a disease called neurofibromatosis—a disorder that can cause everything from learning disabilities to scoliosis to unsightly tumors on a person's skin. The doctors keep close tabs on Thomas, knowing that if his tumor grows or changes, he could lose his sight altogether.

When Nancy first learned of Thomas's condition, she was devastated—and the more she researched the disease, the more her imagination ran wild with the fearsome possibilities. What would the future hold for her precious baby? She was fairly confident she could meet his needs while he was young, but what would happen as he grew? Would his ability to learn be hampered? Would scoliosis prevent him from running and playing with his brothers? Would an outbreak of ugly tumors make him the butt of cruel teenage jokes, wounding his self-esteem and ruining such simple pleasures as an afternoon at the swimming pool?

Most of all, Nancy worried about Thomas's vision. Watching the fireworks one Labor Day weekend, she felt overwhelmed with confusion and uncertainty. *Would Thomas,* she wondered, *be able to enjoy such awesome displays when he got older? Where was God in all of this—and what was he doing?*

Even as Nancy turned these questions over in her mind, God began to reveal his design. Total strangers heard of Thomas's condition and began to pray, and as Thomas grew, no one could deny that God was at work. God had given him, Nancy realized, some unique and incredible gifts. In addition to his outgoing, cheerful personality, Thomas has the spiritual strength, sensitivity, and confidence you would expect to find in a much older person. "He is a great communicator," Nancy says. "God has equipped him with everything he will need— no matter what happens down the road."

Even so, Thomas's crisis is far from over. Each time he has another MRI done or visits another specialist, Rich and Nancy find themselves confronted yet again with uncertainty. But for the two of them—both well-educated, competent people—the questions surrounding Thomas's future have proved to be a blessing in disguise. "We are used to making things happen," Rich says. "With Thomas, though, things are totally out of our control. We can't depend on our own resources. We have to cling to God."

Interestingly enough, in this frank acknowledgment of their human limitations, Rich and Nancy have found a new intimacy with the Lord, as well as a new freedom in parenting. "God," Nancy says, "has taken our worst fears and used them to show us that he is in control. We have no choice but to hold Thomas with an open hand—and really, we ought to have the same perspective of trusting God with respect to all of our kids."

Rich agrees. "Living with complete uncertainty on a daily basis isn't much fun," he says, "but from a faith standpoint, having to trust that God is in control—well, it's a pretty good place to be."

Prayer Principle _____

> The most effective prayers stem from the belief—the unshakable certainty—that God is absolutely, totally, one hundred percent in control.

Poised for Prayer

If your child is in a crisis situation—whether it be because of bad choices she has made, or the result of circumstances beyond his control—don't give up on God. As parenting and family expert James Dobson says, "Even when divine providence seems senseless and contradictory . . . the future belongs to God. He has not forgotten us and his plan has not been thwarted. It is our responsibility . . . to remain faithful and obedient, awaiting His reassurance."[8]

As we await God's reassurance and the unfolding of his plan, we can take courage from the Shunammite woman's example. Let's look again at what she did in response to her crisis:

1. She didn't panic. Instead, she put her trust firmly in God's wisdom and goodness—so much so that she

was able to say that everything was all right, even in her time of pain and loss.

2. She put herself in a place of faith. Rather than surround herself with worriers, skeptics, or mourners, she went straight to Elisha—the one person she knew would understand the situation and see her circumstances through heaven's eyes.

3. She persevered, accepting nothing less than God's best. Emboldened by love for her child, she clung to Elisha's feet, taking refuge in God's presence and refusing to let go.

4. When her answer came, she gave the glory to God. When her son was restored to life, the first thing the Shunammite woman did was fall at Elisha's feet, acknowledging God's power and his grace. She also continued to put her trust in the Lord and live by faith—which, as you can read in 2 Kings 8, saved the lives and fortunes of her entire family when they came face-to-face with another crisis.

If there is a silver lining to be found in crisis situations, it is that they remind us of how much we need God. They break down our notions of self-sufficiency, reveal our inadequacies, and drive us straight into God's arms. My prayer is that, as we face crises of our own, we will respond as the Shunammite woman did: not with our own strength or abilities, but with faith, perseverance, thanksgiving, and trust.

Psalm 121 promises that "he who watches over you will not slumber. . . . The LORD will keep you from all harm—he will watch over your life; the Lord will watch over your coming and going both now and forevermore." If you take just one truth away from this chapter, let it be the knowledge that God is sovereign. He never sleeps; he is always on the watch. He loves you, he loves your children, and he is *always* in control.

Prayers You Can Use

Heavenly Father...

Watch over _____'s life. Do not slumber or sleep, but keep her from all harm. Watch over her life, her coming and going, both now and forevermore. (Psalm 121:3–8)

∾

Do not let anything separate _____ from your love. When trouble, hardship, persecution, danger, or any need arises, let _____ remember that we are "more than conquerors," and that nothing can separate him from the love of God that is in Christ Jesus our Lord. (Romans 8:35–39)

∾

Cause _____ to offer her body as a living sacrifice, holy and pleasing to you, Lord. Let _____ see herself as a temple of the Holy Spirit, belonging to you, that she might flee from sexual immorality and honor you with her body. (Romans 12:1; 1 Corinthians 6:18–20)

∾

*D*o not let _____ be led astray by drugs and alcohol. (Proverbs 20:1)

∾

*K*eep _____ as the apple of your eye; hide him in the shadow of your wings from the wicked who assail him, from mortal enemies who surround him. (Psalm 17:8–9)

∾

*H*em _____ in—behind and before; place your hand upon her so that wherever she goes and whatever she does, she will be accompanied by your presence. (Psalm 139:5–10)

∾

*L*ord, you have summoned _____ by name and he belongs to you. When he passes through the waters, be with him; when he passes through the rivers, do not let them sweep him away. When he walks through the fire, do not let him be burned. And when _____ emerges from these trials, let him know that you are the Lord, that you are his God, that you are the Holy One of Israel, and that you are his Savior. (Isaiah 43:1–3)

∾

*A*s we pray for _____ , do not let us be anxious about anything, but in everything, by prayer and petition, with *thanksgiving, let us always remember to present our requests to you. And let your peace, which transcends all understanding, guard our hearts and our minds in Christ Jesus. (Philippians 4:6–7)*

Part Four

Praying for Your Child's Relationship ...

CHAPTER THIRTEEN

PRAYING FOR YOUR CHILD'S RELATIONSHIPS . . .

WITH FRIENDS

As iron sharpens iron,
so one man sharpens another.

—Proverbs 27:17

ONE OF MY HIGH SCHOOL ENGLISH TEACHERS WOULD ALWAYS HAVE some interesting quotation or kernel of wisdom written in the top right-hand corner of the blackboard. One of my favorites was an old Swedish proverb: *Friendship doubles our joy and divides our grief.* I can still see the words written in her neat cursive hand, and, as I think about the relationships my children forge, the value of having good friends seems greater than ever.

All of us want our kids to have good friends. In addition to the blessings afforded by friendship, it's no secret that, as children grow, few influences hold more sway over their attitude and behavior than the company they keep. As author

Chuck Swindoll puts it, "Close friends become the people you emulate."[1] You don't have to be a psychologist to see the truth in these words, or to recognize the potential down-the-road consequences of the friendships children make. I like the Living Bible's plainspoken rendering of Proverbs 13:21: "Curses chase sinners, while blessings chase the righteous!"

Which group would you want your kids running with?

The good news is that we can influence our children's choice of "running mates." As a teenager I remember my mother taking some rather aggressive steps to ensure that her kids ran with a wholesome crowd—from actions like pulling my sister out of her junior high school to get her away from some "bad" apples to literally pushing me across a crowded restaurant to meet the "good" kids in my high school, seated at a nearby table.

These were the actions my siblings and I saw—and would occasionally cringe at. What we didn't know then was that our parents also spent hours praying for our peers, asking God to surround us with children who loved him, trusting him to use each of us as "salt and light" in the schools we attended.

When I began working on this book, I asked my folks if they would be willing to share any of the many ways God had answered their prayers. Mom immediately e-mailed me a handful of stories, including this one, which I'll let her tell:

> Our family had gone to a camp and had become very enthusiastic Christians. Our oldest daughter loved the fellowship of the other teenagers at the camp, and on weekends she would often ride two hours each way to be with them. She had plenty of friends in her high school, and some of their families attended church, but not one of them had a personal relationship with Jesus Christ.

My husband and I got down on our knees and prayed fervently for a Christian friend for our daughter. We continued to pray fervently for days and weeks, hoping that maybe some Bible-believing family would move to town. But unbeknownst to us, on the first day we began to pray, our next-door neighbors had a meeting at their house with some laypeople and their priest. Someone was asking the church to sponsor a "Life in the Spirit" seminar.

We did not attend the Catholic church, but our daughter heard that this seminar was coming to town, and she invited every one of her high school friends— who were the leaders in the school—to go to it with her. Every one of her best friends received Christ as Savior and they all began a new life together in him. That answer to prayer exceeded abundantly all we could have asked or even imagined!

I was that "oldest daughter," and I have been reaping the benefits of my parents' prayers for my friendships ever since. Reading Mom's e-mail, I couldn't help but smile at the way God had answered their prayers. How many times have I prayed for something—only to watch God answer in a fashion that far exceeded my expectations!

Prayer Principle _____

> God rarely fulfills your expectations when you pray; rather, he tends to exceed them.

A "Two-for-One" Blessing

The picture of my parents asking God to give me a Christian friend reminds me of how God answered my own prayers for our daughter Annesley. When we moved from Atlanta, Georgia, to Winston-Salem, North Carolina, Annesley quickly made many new friends—nice girls both she and I enjoyed having in our home. None of them, however, seemed to share Annesley's passion for the Lord, and I found myself praying for God to give her at least one Christian girl-friend at school—someone whose company would encourage Annesley's faith and strengthen her character.

After more than a year of praying for that "one friend," I was excited when Annesley was invited to join an academic program offered at a nearby school. Maybe, I thought, Annesley would find her "soul mate" there. But as Robbie and I prayed about whether or not to send Annesley to the other school, we sensed God telling us no. The lure of the academic challenge, as well as the possibility for some new friendships, was tempting, but we just couldn't shake the feeling that Annesley was supposed to stay right where she was.

Two days before school started the next fall I discovered the first of several reasons why God wanted Annesley to stay put. We were at the swimming pool, and a friend introduced me to Emily, a woman who had just moved to town. "Emily wants to come to your Friday morning prayer group," my friend said, "and her daughter Emma will be in Annesley's class at school—and look, they've already met each other!"

I looked across the pool and saw Annesley and another girl laughing and splashing in the water. It appeared that their friendship was already in bloom.

"We've been so concerned about how Emma would adjust to a new school," Emily said. "We've been praying for God to give her a Christian friend—you just can't imagine what an answer to prayer Annesley is!"

I had to laugh. "Oh, I can imagine," I replied. "Only, you've got it backwards. It's your daughter Emma who is the answer to prayer!"

Annesley and Emma became good friends. Looking back on the experience, I marvel at the ways God has worked in our lives. He taught Robbie and me a valuable lesson about trusting him and waiting on his timing—even when our human wisdom and common sense were telling us to switch Annesley to a different school. Moreover, by allowing me to pray for more than a year before our answer came, God created an attitude of thankfulness in my heart that might not otherwise have been there had he simply strewn Christian friends in Annesley's path. And finally, I love the picture I now have of God as the master puppeteer, pulling strings in the lives of two families at one time to provide one wonderful answer to prayer.

Prayer Principle _____

> When God doesn't answer your prayers right away, he could be giving you the opportunity to build and demonstrate your faith by waiting on him.

Friendship Is a Two-Way Street

More often than not, our prayers for our children's friendships center around wanting God to provide them with Christian companions. But friendship is a two-way street. All of us want our kids to be surrounded by good influences, but have you ever stopped to consider what sort of friend you want your child to be?

I love the friends who are described in Mark 2:1–12, the passage in which Jesus heals a paralytic. It's not hard to imagine the scene: Jesus had come to town, and when folks heard he was there, they packed the house where he was preaching—so much so that you couldn't even find a spot outside the door.

When four guys showed up with their paralyzed friend, the prospect of getting in to see Jesus must have seemed almost impossible. The press of the crowd, the weight of the stretcher, the dirt and sweat and sore muscles—all these things could easily have conspired to cause them to give up. But, casting their own needs aside, these guys persevered, clawing their way through the roof to get their buddy closer to Jesus. What could have motivated such incredible determination?

Obviously, faith in Jesus' ability to heal must have been the driving factor. But just as important to this story is the fellows' love for their friend. Their tenacity and resourcefulness in bringing the man to Jesus—no matter what it wound up costing them in terms of time, comfort, and convenience—has me sitting at my computer right now, begging God to fill our family with *that* kind of faith, *that* kind of hope, *that* kind of love.

Prayer Principle _____

> Praying for your children's friendships involves praying that
> they will be the kind of friends that you want them to have.

_____ ∾

Poised for Prayer

Praying for our children's friendships, then, calls for a two-pronged approach. First, we must pray that our kids will choose their companions wisely, recognizing—as 1 Corinthians 15:33 so candidly puts it—that "bad company corrupts good character." Our children will undoubtedly be influenced by their peers, so let's ask God to surround them with kids whose lives are marked by integrity, purity, faithfulness, and a vibrant Christian faith. Put another way, we can ask God to give them friends like those described in 2 Timothy 2:22—those who "pursue righteousness, faith, love and peace," and who "call on the Lord out of a pure heart."

Additionally—and with the picture of the paralytic's friends fresh in our minds—we need to ask God to give our children the faithfulness, courage, and determination they will need to be a positive influence for his kingdom. Whether they are at school, playing sports, or simply hanging out with their peers, let's pray for our kids according to Romans 1:16, that they would never be "ashamed of the gospel," but that they would see it as "the power of God for the salvation of everyone who believes." And when they recognize this awesome power, let's pray that our children will be like the paralytic's friends—eager, equipped, and emboldened to "carry" their companions to Jesus.

~ Prayers You Can Use ~

Heavenly Father...

I pray that _____ would choose his friends carefully, for the way of the wicked leads them astray. (Proverbs 12:26 NKJV)

~

Surround _____ with friends who will sharpen her as iron sharpens iron. (Proverbs 27:17)

~

Let _____ flee the evil desires of youth and pursue righteousness, faith, love, and peace, and let him enjoy the companionship of those who call on you out of a pure heart. (2 Timothy 2:22)

~

Bless and keep _____, so that she will not walk in the counsel of the wicked or stand in the way of sinners or sit in the seat of mockers. (Psalm 1:1)

ℬless _____ with friends, and let him be a friend to the friendless, since "two are better than one.... If one falls down, his friend can help him up. But pity the man who falls and has no one to help him up!" (Ecclesiastes 4:9–10)

𝒮hape _____ into a friend who loves at all times. (Proverbs 17:17)

𝒟on't let _____ exclude her peers or participate in gossip, since a perverse person stirs up dissension, and a gossip separates close friends. (Proverbs 16:28)

ℒet _____ seek friendship with you rather than with the world, remembering that anyone who chooses to be a friend of the world becomes your enemy. (James 4:4)

𝒞ount _____ as one of your friends, Lord. Let him live according to your words in John 15:12–14, loving others as you have loved him ... obeying your commands ... and finding his security in the reality of your life-giving love.

CHAPTER FOURTEEN

PRAYING FOR YOUR CHILD'S RELATIONSHIP . . .

WITH SIBLINGS

> How good and pleasant it is
> when brothers live together in unity!
>
> —Psalm 133:1

THAT'S MINE! HE HIT ME! SHE HIT ME FIRST! IT'S NOT FAIR! DO we have to play with her? Go away! No! Yes! No! Yes! No!

Any family that has more than one child has, at some point, experienced the earsplitting agony of sibling conflict. In some families, the clashes are touched off by mundane problems—like who gets to eat the last ice cream sandwich. In others, the issues can run much deeper, such as when two brothers vie for their father's approval.

In our family, as pathetic as it sounds, the number one sibling argument revolves around who gets to sit where in the car. Our Suburban has eight perfectly comfortable seats, but only one has any allure for my kids. They call it "The Corner Seat," and you would think that after five years in the same car, they (or I) would have worked out some sort of seating plan to accommodate everyone. Once I sponsored an essay contest, asking the kids to submit at least three reasons why they liked that particular seat so much, with the prize being a week's worth of sitting in the coveted spot. All I got for my creative parenting was a lengthy poem extolling the virtues of "The Corner Seat" (which, by the way, wound up winning the contest), a colored-pencil portrait of the infamous corner seat (in all its gray, seat-belted beauty), and two loud complaints, filed by the younger kids, who didn't understand the contest rules.

At some point during the Corner Seat Wars, I came upon Matthew 20:20–28. In this passage, James and John and their mother came to Jesus with a request. The mother is the one who actually had the guts to pop the question: "Grant that one of these two sons of mine may sit at your right and the other at your left in your kingdom."

When the other disciples heard what the brothers wanted, they got all bent out of shape—not, I suspect, because they thought the mother's request improper but because they wished they had thought of it first. Here was Jesus, I realized with delight, smack in the middle of a Seat War!

How did the Lord respond? Not the way some of us might have—not, that is, by shouting at the disciples, doling out spankings, or throwing up his hands in disgust over their childish quarrel. Instead, he turned the argument into a teaching tool, pointing out that "whoever wants to become great among you must be your servant."

I love the lessons in this passage. Not only does Jesus' loving response show me how to turn sibling arguments into opportunities for learning, but as a mother, I am encouraged beyond measure to know that the disciples fought! I don't know about you, but there are times when I look at my kids and wonder if they will *ever* stop bickering over who gets to be first, who gets the bigger dessert, or who sits in the corner seat. But when I look at how the disciples turned out— becoming men who gave up their jobs, their reputations, and, in some cases, even their lives for Jesus—it gives me hope that, as my children grow and mature in their relationships with the Lord, he will transform their self-centered squabbles into a genuine desire and ability to put the needs of others before their own.

I don't know why it took the Matthew 20 passage to open my eyes. When God is at work in our children's lives, there is *always* reason to hope. If you are in the place where you are wondering if things will ever get better in your household, my prayer for you comes from Romans 15:13: "May the God of hope fill you with all joy and peace as you trust in him, so that you may overflow with hope by the power of the Holy Spirit."

Prayer Principle _____

Sibling conflicts and rivalries are no match for a parent who knows—and regularly talks to—the God of hope.

A Tale of Two Brothers

Becky could have used a good dose of hope when her boys were young. Jake and Evan weren't even out of diapers before she realized she had her hands full. It seemed that the twins were always fighting—even, Becky remembered with a grimace, before they were born. She imagined she could still feel the kicks and punches that the boys threw at each other in her womb.

As they grew, the differences became more obvious. Jake liked to hang around the house and help Becky in the kitchen, while Evan could hardly wait to get outdoors every day, no matter how bad the weather. He loved to fashion guns and knives out of the sticks in his yard, and he dreamed of the day when he could go deer hunting with his dad. As a result, Becky found herself drawn to the quiet-natured Jake, while Evan won a special place in his father's heart.

The fact that their parents played favorites was not lost on the boys. And the teenage years only accentuated their rivalry: A well-conditioned outdoorsman, Evan was stronger and faster than his brother, and he was by far the superior marksman. But Jake was not discouraged; more often than not, he found he could outsmart his burly sibling—and if his wits ever failed him, he was not above using trickery or lies to get his own way.

Becky sensed a showdown coming. Her elderly husband was in failing health, and she knew that the old man had recently revised his will to leave the bulk of his estate—including a controlling interest in the family business—to Jake. When Evan learned of the change, he was livid—and consoled himself with the thought of eventually killing his twin.

You've probably guessed by now that Jake and Evan are not these boys' real names. In reality, they are Jacob and Esau, the sons of Isaac and Rebekah. After Jacob wrangled both the birthright and his father's blessing away from his minutes-older twin, he had to run for his life, lest Esau make good on his murderous vow. Their decades-long conflict makes most of today's sibling squabbles pall in comparison.[1]

And yet look what happened to these brothers: Twenty years after Jacob fled, he returned to his homeland, accompanied by his wives, children, and flocks. Esau went out to meet him and took along four hundred able-bodied men. Jacob must have feared the worst, because he put his favorite wife, Rachel, and son, Joseph, in the very back of his procession, where they might gain a measure of protection from Esau's all-but-certain assault.[2]

But then the incredible happened. When Esau saw Jacob, he ran to him, threw his arms around him, and kissed him. The brothers wept in each other's arms!

Why the big change? What happened to Esau's violent intentions and the grudge he must have been nursing for years? The Bible makes no mention of an intervention on Isaac or Rebekah's part. Nor does it say Jacob ever apologized for deceiving his brother; in fact, the "I'm sorry" is conspicuously absent in the narrative. All we know is that, as he prepared to meet Esau, Jacob was shaking in his boots.

And so Jacob turned to God: "Save me, I pray, from the hand of my brother Esau, for I am afraid he will come and attack me, and also the mothers with their children. But you have said, 'I will surely make you prosper and will make your descendants like the sand of the sea, which cannot be counted.'"[3]

Prayer works. In this case, it changed Esau's heart and made an unthinkable reunion possible. When we follow Jacob's lead and use God's promises as the anchor for our prayers, we can be confident that he will respond. As Psalm 145:13 says, "The LORD is faithful to all his promises and loving toward all he has made."

Prayer Principle

When you pray according to God's promises,
you can expect him to keep them.

A Tale of Two Sisters

Mary had always wanted a sister. The relationships she observed between her friends and *their* sisters seemed so special, and Mary sensed she had missed something growing up with only a brother for companionship. Thus, when her daughter was born, she quickly put in her request: "Please, God," she prayed, "can I have another one?"

Mary's prayer was answered, and, as her daughters grew, their relationship was everything she had ever envisioned. Just two years apart in age, Sarah and Libby spent endless hours playing dolls, inventing games and secret codes, and sharing each other's dreams and joys. "Thank you, God," Mary whispered to herself, hardly daring to hope that the magic would last.

Sometime after Sarah's eighth birthday, the cracks began to appear. Sarah had made several new friends at school, and

169

she had made it clear that Libby was not welcome in their circle. Almost before she knew what was happening, Mary felt like her home had turned into a war zone. "I kept praying for their relationship," she told me, "but the girls wanted nothing to do with each other. It broke my heart."

No one, though, felt the strain more keenly than the girls themselves. Each summer they spent a month at a Christian camp, where they were surrounded by what seemed like a million pairs of happy sisters. "My sister is my best friend," one camper said. Sarah could hardly believe her ears. Who ever heard of sisters being best friends? The girl might as well have said that her sister was an iguana.

Even so, Sarah and Libby had to admit that they were envious of the other girls' relationships. Rather than own up to their differences, though, they opted to put on a show, pretending to enjoy one another's company so as to fit in with the other campers. They both knew it was a farce—and that as soon as they got home, they would pick up their battle shields once again.

Finally Sarah went off to college. Mary relished the newfound peace that marked her home, but her heart's cry remained unchanged. Her constant prayer was for the girls to enjoy a real relationship—one that went beyond public masks and temporary truces. The fact that she had two girls was an answer to her specific prayer—of that she was certain. If only God would intervene and knit their hearts together!

What Mary did not know was that God *was* at work. Sarah and Libby graduated from college and eventually found themselves living in the same town. Away from home, with only each other for "family," they forged an alliance of sorts that, given time, grew into a full-fledged friendship. Sarah's faith was also growing, and one day she sent Mary a copy of a devotional she had written. The general theme dealt with her relationship with God, but tucked into the lesson were two sentences that grabbed Mary's attention:

> I can now say, with a candor that I reserve for the most serious of affairs, that I love my sister more than any other person on earth. She is not only my best friend, but also my greatest human source of strength.

Mary read the devotional over and over again. Seemingly out of nowhere her prayers had been answered: Her daughters were best friends! Mary's heart felt like it might break all over again, this time with heartfelt gratitude. God, she realized, had been there all the time.

Prayer Principle _____

> God hears your prayers, and he is always at work—
> even when you cannot see what he is doing.

Poised for Prayer

Sarah and Libby's childhood differences are far more common than either of them might imagine. Even in Christ-centered homes, factors such as competitive personalities, the illusion (or reality) of parental favoritism, and our sinful human nature make conflict almost impossible to avoid. As evidenced by the tension that marked Cain and Abel's relationship, sibling rivalry has been around as long as siblings have![4]

My own daughters are a case in point. Annesley is just a year behind Hillary in school, and she is always nipping at her heels. When Hillary learned to read, Annesley paid close attention—and quickly taught herself the same trick. When Hillary took up soccer, Annesley strapped on her cleats and followed suit. And when Hillary landed in the family spotlight after losing a baby tooth one night, Annesley immediately yanked out one of her own, emerging minutes later with her bloody trophy in hand!

As a result of these antics, I have been keenly aware of the need to pray for their relationship. And although they still squabble (especially about "The Corner Seat"), I know God has heard my prayers. One night as I was tucking the girls into bed after practicing multiplication facts with them, Hillary said, "Annesley, you know your math facts so much better than I do." I could hear the discouragement in Hillary's voice, and as I poked around in my brain for an effective way to salvage her self-esteem, Annesley stepped into the gap: "Only because *you* taught them to me, Hillary."

Thank you, Lord! Today it's math facts; tomorrow the minefield may involve more significant issues. But because God has been faithful with the little things, I know he will handle the big ones.

If your children are young, don't wait until they start sparring to cover their relationship with prayer. Be proactive, using verses like the ones listed below to lift them before God's throne, trusting that when conflicts crop up, God can take what Satan intends for evil and turn it to your children's advantage.

If your children are older, and strong sibling ties are nothing but a distant memory or an abandoned vision, don't give up. Follow Mary's example. Bathe them in prayer, recognize that God often works in unseen ways, and remember that he *always* keeps his promises.

Prayers You Can Use

Heavenly Father...

Give _____ *and his siblings endurance, encouragement, and a spirit of unity as they follow Christ Jesus, so that with one heart and mouth they may glorify you, precious Lord. (Romans 15:5–6)*

❧

Do not let any unwholesome talk come out of _____*'s mouth, but only what is helpful for building others up according to their needs, that it may benefit those who listen. (Ephesians 4:29)*

❧

Cause _____ *and her siblings to be devoted to one another in brotherly love, honoring one another above themselves. (Romans 12:10)*

❧

173

*L*et _____ love his siblings, for love comes from you. Remind him that everyone who loves has been born of God and knows God, and that whoever loves God must also love his brother. (1 John 4:7, 21)

❧

I pray that _____ will do everything without arguing or complaining. (Philippians 2:14)

❧

*L*et _____ and her siblings be encouraged and knit together with strong ties of love. Let them have the rich experience of knowing Christ with real certainty and clear understanding. (Colossians 2:2 LB)

❧

*D*o not permit _____ to be quarrelsome; instead, cause him to be gentle, patient, and humble, especially when his siblings are in the wrong ... because then they will be more likely, with God's help, to turn away from their wrong ideas and believe what is true. (2 Timothy 2:24–26 LB)

❧

*L*et _____ live in harmony with her siblings, being sympathetic, compassionate, and humble. Don't let _____ and her siblings repay evil with evil or insult with insult, but with blessing. (1 Peter 3:8–9)

❧

Help _____ to control his temper, since anyone who is angry with his brother will be subject to judgment. If _____ holds anything against one of his siblings, prompt him to go and be reconciled so that he may have fellowship with you. (Matthew 5:22–24)

❧

Show _____ and her siblings how to be kind and compassionate to one another, forgiving each other, just as you forgave them. (Ephesians 4:32)

❧

Make our home a good and pleasant place, where brothers (and sisters!) live together in unity. (Psalm 133:1)

CHAPTER FIFTEEN

PRAYING FOR YOUR CHILD'S RELATIONSHIP . . .

WITH TEACHERS AND COACHES

Obey your leaders and submit to their authority.
They keep watch over you as men who must give an account.
Obey them so that their work will be a joy, not a burden,
for that would be of no advantage to you.

— Hebrews 13:17

I'LL NEVER FORGET THE DAY ONE OF OUR DAUGHTERS CAME HOME from school and announced that her new teacher was a Christian.

I looked up from the manuscript I was proofreading, intrigued. "Really?" I asked. "How do you know?"

"I know she's a Christian because she prays," came the reply.

"She prays?"

"Yes, Mom. Almost every day she says, 'O God, help me get through this day.' But sometimes she just says, 'O God,' and puts her head down on her desk."

I laugh every time I remember that story, and my heart still goes out to that teacher!

Like so many parents, Robbie and I prayed long and hard about where to send our children to school. We lived in Atlanta when the time came to enroll Hillary in kindergarten, and we clearly sensed God leading us to send her to the local public school. Despite some of our concerns about the general state of public education (especially in a big city), we obeyed this prompting. Later, when we moved to Winston-Salem, we revisited the issue and again felt drawn to the public school. We knew—as we had in Atlanta—that not all of our children's teachers would be Christians, and that some might be directly opposed to our faith. Yet we couldn't deny what God had told us to do, and so, following the advice of Proverbs 3:5–6, we decided to trust God instead of leaning on our own understanding, and to rely on him to make our paths straight.

And he has. We have been blessed with wonderful teachers, wise administrators, and an education that has exceeded our highest expectations, both academically and in terms of how the experience has shaped our children's characters. Every spring we pray that God will choose our kids' teachers for the following year, and while we have not always gotten the teacher *we* would have chosen, God, in his infinite wisdom, has proved that *he* knows what is best for our kids.

My friend Camille, who also asks God to pick her children's teachers, loves the freedom inherent in this approach. "Instead of agonizing over which teacher our kids will get, we just leave it up to God. He knows their needs better than anyone."

Praying that God will choose your child's teachers—and then living with his answers—is not always easy. One year, for instance, one of our daughters wound up in a class with a teacher whose academic standards were not very high, and we worried that she would be bored or lose interest in school. In hindsight, though, we realized what God knew all along: Our daughter's greatest need that year was not for intellectual stimulation but for emotional acceptance—and the love and praise she received from this particular teacher built her self-confidence in a way that academic challenges never could have.

Prayer Principle _____

Asking God to choose your children's teachers frees you from having to worry about or meddle in the decision.

The Life-Changing Power of Prayer

I am not, of course, advocating a "hands-off" approach to your children's education. There will undoubtedly be times when you have concerns and you will want to meet with the teacher or the principal. But before you start worrying, complaining, or maneuvering, ask God if there is anything else he wants you to do.

Sharon's daughter, Addy, was a model student, popular with her teachers as well as with her classmates. Thus, when a high school math teacher went out of her way to make Addy's life miserable, Sharon and Addy couldn't help but wonder what God was thinking.

The teacher, Mary Ellen, was a single woman who had grown up under the shadows of divorce, poverty, and a physically abusive, tyrannical father. She really knew very little about God, but her parents' religious community adhered to incredibly strict rules and used fear and punishment to perpetuate their faith—distorting her concept of a loving, heavenly Father.

Years later, when Mary Ellen became a math teacher, her longtime distrust of anything religious manifested itself in the way she treated her students, particularly those she identified as "Christians." She ridiculed their beliefs and bullied them into questioning their convictions—so much so that Addy and her friends would come home from school in tears.

One day Sharon got a call from the school secretary, who knew that Sharon and several other moms prayed for their children and for the school in an informal prayer group each week. "Mary Ellen is having hip surgery next week," she said, "and she's not doing very well. She expects all of us here at school to take care of her, but we have families of our own. I don't know how she'll manage—she has nobody, you know. Could you ask your group to pray for her?"

Sharon agreed to pray—yet inwardly cringed. She did not like Mary Ellen, they had nothing in common, and, if truth be told, she didn't much care what happened to the woman. Nevertheless, she and her group began to pray, and as they did, the women began to sense God leading them to take care of the teacher. Like Sharon, none of the mothers felt at all close to Mary Ellen, and providing the physical support she would need would be more than just an inconvenience: Not only did Mary Ellen live far away, but her apartment was on the third floor—and the thought of three flights' worth of complaining and Christian-bashing as they helped her go up and down was more than any of them could bear.

Even so, the mothers accepted their assignment, driving Mary Ellen to the hospital, sitting with her at her bedside, and cooking and caring for her as she recuperated at home. Desperate for help, Mary Ellen could do little but receive their gesture—although she was quick to remind them that she thought that their prayers were a big waste of time.

In time, though, Mary Ellen's heart began to soften. Sitting with her one day, Sharon had the privilege of sharing the gospel—the *real* message of God's love—and then praying with the teacher as she committed her life to Jesus Christ. Addy and the other students who knew what their mothers were doing watched in amazement as Mary Ellen returned to school, obviously a changed person. Even the other teachers noticed.

"Watch out for those moms in that prayer group," one of her coworkers warned. "They're in some kind of a cult."

"You may think that," Mary Ellen calmly replied, "but they are the first people I've ever met who really loved me."

Today, Mary Ellen is one of Sharon's good friends, and she has spent a number of Christmases with Sharon and Addy's family. And because Sharon and the other moms acted out of obedience to God—rather than on the basis of their feelings—they have all learned a valuable lesson. "Our kids will have tough teachers," Sharon told me, "but trying to protect them from these situations is not always the wisest course. Sometimes God allows a difficult situation just so they can see his power to change people."

Prayer Principle _____

> Praying for your children's teachers—instead of complaining about them—will encourage your kids to rely on God's power in the face of difficult circumstances.

_____ ∼

Praying for a Teachable Spirit

If you're like me, you tend to spend more time praying for your kids to get the right *teachers* than that they will be the right *students*. But how our children think and behave in the classroom or on the athletic field can go farther toward fostering strong relationships with teachers and coaches than just about anything else.

Ned and Drew are two of the most teachable young men I know. Eager learners, they are quick to explore new ideas, and they have learned to recognize and respect the giftedness of their teachers—even when some of the concepts they were taught clashed with their own Christian convictions.

Ned and Drew's willingness to learn is also evident in their athletic pursuits. Both are outstanding runners, a trait they inherited from their father, Jim, an Olympic medalist who was the first high schooler to run a mile in less than four minutes. When Ned and Drew won spots on their high school track team, Jim vowed not to interfere with the coach's methods. Moreover, he encouraged his sons to respect the coach's authority, even if the man's coaching style differed from their father's teaching.

As it turned out, the high school track coach did not do everything the way the former Olympian would have, and Ned and Drew knew it. But rather than argue with the man or rebel against his methods, the boys opted to buckle down and do their very best, while Jim and his wife, Anne, stayed content to pray for their sons from the bleachers. As a result of the family's gentle, teachable spirit, the coach saw Christianity in a very favorable light—a testimony that would not have been possible had Ned and Drew taken an aggressive or defiant stand against his techniques. What's more, the track team won an unprecedented (and never-repeated) series of three straight state championships.

Every life has its share of boredom, dissatisfaction, frustration, and tragedy. But if our children can learn to meet each new challenge, as Ned and Drew did, by seeing the value in other people, respecting authority, and looking for opportunities to learn and grow, then even painful or disappointing circumstances can become reasons for thanksgiving. And long after our children have graduated from classrooms and playing fields, a teachable spirit will prove its lasting worth in their careers, their marriages, and their ability to minister to others.

Prayer Principle _____

> Asking God to give your children a teachable spirit involves allowing him to use their mistakes and failures as stepping-stones on the path to victory.

Poised for Prayer

Our children aren't the only ones who need a teachable spirit. As parents, we must adopt a similar attitude of gratitude and respect—particularly when we approach our kids' teachers, coaches, or school administrators. I learned this lesson the hard way when I told a teacher what I thought was wrong with a book she had recommended to one of our kids—without first giving her the chance to explain why she liked the story so much. When I finally got around to considering her point of view, I realized that some of her ideas made sense—but my opportunity for sharing a Christian perspective on the subject matter was long gone.

If you find your kids (or yourself) in a tough spot with a teacher or a coach, don't criticize the teacher—especially not in front of your children. Instead, make prayer your top priority. Praying for your children's teachers can soften your heart toward them and cause you to see them as God sees them: as his precious children, regardless of where they are in their journey of faith. Invite your children to join you in this work, and don't get discouraged if you don't see an immediate change. Focus on verses like 1 Corinthians 15:58, which reminds us to stand firm and give ourselves "fully to the work of the Lord, because you know that your labor in the Lord [that is, your prayer] is not in vain."

Next, check your attitude. Get rid of defensiveness, self-righteousness, bitterness, or anger, replacing those traits with humility, gentleness, gratitude, and love. Ask God to give you and your kids a teachable spirit, and diligently follow Paul's advice in Colossians 4:6: "Let your conversation be always full of grace, seasoned with salt, so that you may know how to answer everyone."

Finally, remember that you are part of a bigger picture. When your child graduates from a classroom or a school, God will likely bring another Christian family into that classroom or school to take your place. Don't say or do anything to jeopardize that family's testimony; *you* might not have to live with the consequences of your actions, but *they* will. Instead, think of yourselves as runners in a race, receiving the baton from those who have gone before you and passing it on to those who follow.

Jesus said that the "harvest is plentiful but the workers are few."[1] How our families minister to our teachers is, from a kingdom perspective, just as important as how they impact us. Let's learn to see our teachers and our schools as harvest fields, and let's thank God for giving us—and all those who come behind us—the privilege of working alongside him to bring in the harvest.

Prayers You Can Use

Heavenly Father...

Turn ____'s ear toward wisdom and her heart toward understanding. Give her a teachable spirit, one that calls out for insight and searches for it as for hidden treasure. (Proverbs 2:2–4)

❧

*C*ause _____ to obey his teachers and coaches and submit to their authority. Let him know that these people keep watch over him and that you will hold them accountable for the job they do. Show _____ that when he obeys his teachers and coaches and makes their work a joy instead of a burden, the end result will be to his advantage. (Hebrews 13:17)

❧

*M*ake _____ and her teachers completely humble and gentle. Let them be patient, bearing with one another in love. (Ephesians 4:2)

❧

I pray that _____ would show proper respect to everyone. Let him love his brothers and sisters in Christ, fear you, and honor those in authority over him. (1 Peter 2:17)

❧

*D*on't let any teacher take _____ captive through hollow and deceptive philosophy, which depends on human tradition and the basic principles of this world rather than on Christ. (Colossians 2:8)

❧

*L*et _____'s teachers and coaches never become weary in doing good, but let them know that at the proper time they will reap a harvest if they do not give up. Likewise, don't let _____ grow weary as she prays for her teachers. (Galatians 6:9)

∾

*C*ause _____ to be wise in the way he acts toward his teachers, making the most of every opportunity. Let his conversation be always full of grace, seasoned with salt, so that he will know how to respectfully and graciously answer his teachers' questions. (Colossians 4:5–6)

∾

*Y*ou know our needs even before we ask you, Lord, and you promise to work in all things for the good of those who love you. Handpick each one of _____'s teachers, and surround her with classmates of your choosing. (Matthew 6:8; Romans 8:28)

∾

*R*emind _____ to pray for his teachers and coaches and give thanks for the role they play in his life. (1 Timothy 2:1–2)

∾

I pray that _____'s male teachers and coaches would be men of temperance, dignity, and wisdom, with lives marked by faith, love, and endurance. I pray that the women in _____'s life would be models of goodness, self-control, reverence, and purity. In everything, let these men and women set an example for _____ by doing what is good. (Titus 2:2–7)

CHAPTER SIXTEEN

PRAYING FOR YOUR CHILD'S RELATIONSHIP . . .

WITH YOU

Honor your father and your mother, as the LORD your God has
commanded you, so that you may live long and that it may go well
with you in the land the LORD your God is giving you.

—Deuteronomy 5:16

YEARS AGO, WHEN OUR TWO OLDER DAUGHTERS WERE VERY YOUNG,
I remember being frustrated at their failure to obey me. I can't
recall their particular offense, but I will never forget the conversation we had afterwards, sitting together on one of their beds.

"It makes me so sad when you disobey me," I said.

"Don't be sad, Mommy. We love you!" Hillary replied.

"If you love me," I countered, "you should obey me."

Before the words were even out of my mouth, it hit me—
Jesus said essentially the same thing to his disciples in John
14:15: "If you love me, you will obey what I command."

As I contemplated the parallel sentiments, it occurred to me that God must feel the same disappointment when I disobey him that I feel when my kids don't do what I ask them to do. I turned the idea over in my mind a few times and then found myself voicing my next thoughts out loud. "Girls," I said, "I'm not trying to be mean or unfair when I ask you to obey me. Daddy and I love you. So does God. And there will come a time when God tells you to do something. If you haven't learned to obey Daddy and me, how will you know how to obey God?"

"Jonah didn't obey God," Annesley said solemnly.

"Exactly!" I blurted out, grateful to be handed such a fitting illustration. *"And look what happened to him!"*

James Dobson says that a child's "early view of parental authority becomes the cornerstone of his future outlook on school authority, law enforcement officers, employers, and others with whom he will eventually live and work."[1] This concept makes sense to me, and, although I'm no psychologist, I'd venture to say that a child's relationship with his parents also plays a major role in setting the stage for his eventual relationship with God. If he learns to love, trust, and obey his parents, he will have an easier time reaching this level of intimacy with his heavenly Father.

Maybe that's why the parent-child relationship seems to matter so much to God. When he gave Moses the Ten Commandments, the one about honoring your father and mother was the only one that came with a promise attached: "Honor your father and your mother, so that you may live long in the land the LORD your God is giving you."[2] Deuteronomy

5:16 restates this commandment and includes the phrase "and that it may go well with you."

When we pray for our children's relationship with us, we invite God to unleash his blessings in their lives, fulfilling his promise that things "may go well" with them. What a privilege it is to know that our expressions of love for our children can pave the way for God to reveal himself as their heavenly Father!

Prayer Principle _____

> Praying for your children to love, respect, trust, and obey you helps pave the way for them to love, respect, trust, and obey their heavenly Father.

Loving Your Kids When You Don't Feel Like It

God wants children to honor and obey their parents, but his plan for family relationships doesn't end there. The Bible is full of verses that point to a parent's duty to properly manage his or her household—including Titus 2:3–5, in which Paul exhorts the older women to train the younger women "to love their husbands and children."

At first glance, Paul's charge seems rather odd. After all, how do you *train* somebody to love? And do mothers really need advice and urging when it comes to loving their kids?

I think so—or at least, I think there are times when we could use a little help. As I began working on this book, several of the mothers I spoke with confessed that it was sometimes difficult for them to *like* all of their children—regardless of how much they *loved* them. But that's where stories like Beth's are instructive. At age forty-six, Beth is hardly the picture of a wise old woman, but she definitely qualifies as a personal trainer under the Titus 2 guidelines.

Beth has eight children, and in her twenty-plus years of motherhood, she has experienced more than one bump along the way. One of her children, in particular, proved tougher to love than his siblings. As a youngster, Justin was easygoing and compliant, but as he reached his teenage years, his personality revealed a new side. The more Beth tried to love him, the more he pulled away—and before Beth or her husband, Tim, knew what was happening, they found themselves separated from their son by an almost impossibly wide chasm. No matter what they said or did, Justin managed to find fault. It was almost a relief when he opted to join the military rather than finish school; at least Beth and Tim wouldn't have to face his rebellion and condemnation on a daily basis.

But eventually Justin came home—bringing a wife with him. She carried a chip on her shoulder almost identical to his, and Beth and Tim wound up walking on eggshells in Justin's presence, lest they say or do something that might offend him.

As Beth prayed about her relationship with Justin, she realized that she couldn't hold herself responsible for Justin's actions or his feelings. Her job was simply to love him and let

God handle the rest. Moreover, God showed Beth that the typical way she showed love to her family—in things like love notes and chocolate kisses left on their pillows—wouldn't necessarily be the "flavor" of love that would appeal to Justin or penetrate his prickly heart.

"Show me how to love Justin, Lord," Beth prayed. "I confess that I don't *feel* like loving him—but I am willing to let my head rule our relationship, rather than my heart."

As Beth continued to pray—willing herself to show love, regardless of Justin's response—an incredible thing happened. Her heart began, she says, to "grow up to" her head, and she began to experience a deep and genuine *liking* for her son, as well as for his wife. By consciously choosing to obey God and show love to her son—even when he didn't seem to deserve it, or even want it—Beth opened the door to her heart and allowed God to go to work.

"I know it's been said before," Beth told me, "but God really *can* turn awful circumstances into good ones, if we are willing to let him—and if we're willing to obey him, no matter how we feel."

Prayer Principle _____

Love is a decision, not an emotion. Prayerfully purposing to follow your head rather than your heart can help you love your children—even when they act more like porcupines than people.

Setting an Example

Joanna is one of our favorite baby-sitters. She recently got married, and during all of the wedding preparations and festivities, I was amazed by the closeness that she and her mother, Myrtie, shared. I've known a lot of loving mothers and daughters, but even the best mother-daughter relationships can buckle a bit when wedding plans are being made. How, I wondered, did Myrtie get such a great daughter? How did Joanna get such a great mom?

Myrtie would never boast about her relationship with Joanna—or with her two sons, for that matter—but I begged her to let me share part of a note that Joanna had sent her in a birthday card one year. I think it offers a clue to the strength of their mother-daughter love and provides a worthwhile lesson as to how we should pray for our own parent-child relationships:

> You have lived your life for God and have been a flawless example to all your children. Thank you for being such a role model for me as I have gradually become a woman, will soon become a wife, and will someday become a mother. Without your guidance, steadfast example, and ceaseless prayers, I don't know where I'd be.

Reading Joanna's words, I found myself looking toward the future and praying that my daughters would one day feel this same way about me. But along with this prayer comes a strong sense of my own responsibility: that of setting a godly example for my children.

We all want to be a good example for our kids—but how often do we stop and consider what it really entails? In addition to changing diapers, running car pools, and helping with science projects, godly women are supposed to be wise, resourceful, hospitable, encouraging, diligent, creative, generous, faithful, watchful, vigorous, strong, and cheerful—and that's just for starters! If you think I'm making this up, take a look at Proverbs 31.

Reading this passage used to discourage me. I'd start by checking off the verses I had "covered"—things like sewing curtains and dust-ruffles, or keeping my lamp burning late into the night as I made endless "To Do" lists. But no matter how hard I tried, I never got much farther than that. I was always, as my friend Kenzie likes to put it, "the Proverbs 32 woman."

But that's where Jesus comes in. By myself I will never measure up. No matter how hard I try to do everything "right," there will always be times when I let my children down. Unlike the Proverbs 31 mother, I will probably never know what it feels like to have my kids get out of bed in the morning and call me "blessed!" But I have learned that the less I rely on my own abilities and the more I rely on Christ—and the more I let my children see me depending on him for wisdom, guidance, and strength—the more I will be able to set an example that's worth following. Instead of saying, "Look at me," I'll be able to say, "Look at Jesus."

Myrtie is a great mom, and she's one of the kindest and most generous and loving women I know. But she is also human, and Joanna—like daughters everywhere—is undoubtedly well aware of her mother's faults. When Joanna calls Myrtie a "flawless example," I don't think she means that her mother is perfect. Instead, I suspect that when Joanna looks at her mother, what she really sees is a reflection of Jesus.

Prayer Principle _____

> When your children see your prayerful dependence on
> the Lord, they will learn to look past your weaknesses to
> recognize and appreciate God's strengths.

_____ ∾

Poised for Prayer

What do your kids see when they look at you? If you are
where I was—trying to earn your kids' love and your husband's praise by being the Proverbs 31 woman—give it up.
You can't do it. *But God can.* God can make you the wife and
mother he wants you to be, just as he can shape and develop
your children in answer to your prayers.

As you allow God to work in your life, find an older
woman whose relationship with her children is very much like
the one you want for your own family. Watch what she does,
and then, like the younger women in Titus 2, follow her lead,
turning your observations into prayers. When I look at Myrtie
and Joanna's relationship, for example, three specific prayers
come to mind:

1. *I ask God to give me time with my kids, as well as an
   eagerness on the part of all of us to spend time
   together.* Myrtie has invested countless hours with her
   children, from crawling around on the floor with them
   when they were little to taking them on long bike trips

when they grew up—and it shows. Again and again I have seen her put relationships ahead of "To Do" lists, and I pray that God will show me how to use my time so wisely.

2. *I ask God to help me see discipline as a gift rather than as a necessary evil.* The limits that Myrtie imposed on her kids' behavior while they were growing up were not always popular. But, as she once told me, "you have to be willing for your kids not to like you at any given moment in order to prove to them that you really do love them. Children find security in limits—and they won't feel as loved if they are always allowed to do anything they want."

3. *I ask God to show me how to point my kids toward Jesus Christ.* Things like time, discipline, and love are all part of a strong parent-child relationship, but, Myrtie says, "the most important thing you can do for your kids is to show and tell them about God's love." I pray that as I point my kids toward Christ, and that as they grow closer to him, we will also grow closer to each other.

These are some of my prayers; you will undoubtedly discover others as you study the lives and methods of women who have walked the motherhood road ahead of you. The main thing is to pray—both for your children and for yourself—so that as you follow God's commands, you and your children will reap the benefits of a stronger, healthier, more enjoyable relationship with each other.

Prayers You Can Use

Heavenly Father...

Cause _____ *to obey us, for this is right. Let him honor us, his father and his mother, so that it may go well with him and that he may enjoy a long life on earth. (Ephesians 6:1–3)*

∾

Don't let us exasperate _____; *instead, help us bring her up in the training and instruction of the Lord. (Ephesians 6:4)*

∾

Let _____ *listen to his father's instruction, and never forsake his mother's teaching. Let* _____ *love wisdom and therefore bring joy to our hearts. (Proverbs 1:8; 29:3)*

∾

Teach _____ *to obey us in everything, for this pleases you, Lord. Do not let us do or say anything that would embitter or discourage her. (Colossians 3:20–21)*

∾

You promise to tend your flock like a shepherd. Gather _____ like a lamb in your arms and carry him close to your heart. And, just as you promise to gently lead those that have young, teach us, as parents, how to lead and guide and care for _____ . (Isaiah 40:11)

∾

Let _____ keep our commands and never forsake our teaching. Let her bind them upon her heart forever and fasten them around her neck. When she walks, let our teaching guide her; when she sleeps, let it watch over her; when she wakes, let our words speak to her. Let _____ regard our instruction and our commands as a guiding lamp; let her welcome our correction as the way to life. (Proverbs 6:20–23)

∾

Let us learn to see discipline as a gift. Let _____ recognize that when we discipline him, it means that we love him and that he belongs to our family—just as you discipline those you love, those you accept as your sons and daughters. Let _____ respect us when we discipline him, realizing that we are doing our best and that we ourselves are submitting to your discipline, which is for our good. (Hebrews 12:5–10)

∾

Turn our hearts toward our children, and our children's hearts toward us. (Malachi 4:6)

∾

Let us love one another with the love that comes from you. And as we love each other, live in us, Lord, and make your love complete in us. (1 John 4:7, 12)

Part Five

Praying for Your Child's Future

CHAPTER SEVENTEEN

PRAYING FOR YOUR CHILD'S PURPOSE IN LIFE

"For I know the plans I have for you," declares the LORD, "plans to prosper you and not to harm you, plans to give you hope and a future."

—Jeremiah 29:11

AS I WAS WORKING ON THIS BOOK ONE NIGHT—I CAN'T BELIEVE I'M telling you this story—I heard one of our children creeping up the back stairs that lead to my office. "Who's there?" I called.

"It's Virginia," came the soft reply.

"You're supposed to be asleep!" I snapped, never taking my eyes off the computer screen. "It's way past your bed-time—get back to bed *right now!*"

I heard Virginia turn and scuttle back down the steps. Then, when she was almost out of earshot, her little voice came floating back: "But I've been waiting for you to come and pray with me!"

To say that I felt like a dirty dog would be an understatement. Robbie was out of town on business, and I had hustled the children into bed earlier in the evening, promising to come back to kiss them good night and pray with them "in a minute." As I tidied up the kitchen, returned a few phone calls, and sat down at the computer—totally forgetting my promise—that minute had stretched into more than an hour. There I was, diligently looking up Bible verses on prayer—and leaving the actual praying undone! The fact that I practically bit Virginia's head off when she interrupted my efforts only made a bad situation worse.

By contrast, consider how my friend, Hollis, handled a similar interruption. Hollis often wakes up early in the morning to spend time with the Lord. She has this wonderfully big four-poster bed, stocked with plenty of goose down pillows and piles of comfortable linens and blankets, and I can picture her sitting there at 5:30 A.M., wrapped in her bathrobe, with a steaming mug of Cafe Vienna in one hand and her Bible propped open on her lap.

On one such morning, Hollis heard a creak on the floorboards. Moments later, her daughter, Sarah Lawton, quietly slipped into the room. "What are you doing, Mommy?" Sarah Lawton asked.

"Reading my Bible."

"What are you reading?"

"Well," Hollis said, setting her coffee on her bedside table, "come and see."

Sarah Lawton clambered up into the big bed and snuggled into her mother's arms.

Hollis picked up where she had left off, softly reading the words from Jeremiah 29:11–13. "'For I know the plans I have for you,' declares the LORD, 'plans to prosper you and not to harm you, plans to give you hope and a future. Then you will call upon me and come and pray to me, and I will listen to you. You will seek me and find me when you seek me with all your heart.'"

As she read, Hollis was struck with the realization of how these verses must have sounded to her daughter. "Sarah Lawton," she said, "did you know that these words were written for you? God has a special plan for your life and a special purpose for your future. And he promises that when you look for him, you will find him."

Parenting experts tell us to take advantage of such "teachable moments" in our children's lives. Hollis gave her daughter a sense of destiny, value, and purpose—simply by including her in her Bible study. How much better it would have been had I heard Virginia on the stairs and welcomed her into my office, showing her the verses I had found and telling her—as Hollis had told Sarah Lawton—that God's promises were written especially for her.

God loves your children, and he has a special plan for each of their lives. But your opportunities for communicating these truths won't always come when you want them to or in the manner you expect them to. In this chapter, I want to open your eyes to the ways you can pray for your child's sense of his or her purpose in life, and encourage you to be alert to the "teachable moments" that God places in your days.

Prayer Principle _____

> You can pray for your children's future with hope and
> confidence, knowing that God loves them and has a
> special plan for each of their lives.

_____ ∿

God Uses Ordinary People

God gave me one such unexpected moment a few weeks
ago at Hillary's tenth birthday party. It was her first slumber
party, and as I helped nine young girls arrange their sleeping
bags in Hillary's room, I suddenly decided to tell them a bed-
time story. "How many of you," I asked, "have ever heard
of Queen Esther?"

Esther, I figured, was a prime candidate for a group of pre-
teen girls. Her story is full of romance, intrigue, murderous
plots, danger, and triumph. Not only that, but Esther—as
beautiful as she was—had to complete twelve months of
beauty treatments before she could appear before the king. If
all that stuff about perfumes and cosmetics didn't appeal to
the ten-year-old female mind, I didn't know what would!

Esther was also, the Bible tells us, an ordinary Jewish girl
who had been orphaned at a young age and raised by her cousin,
Mordecai. It wasn't until she landed in the palace that God put
into motion his ultimate plan for her life—and what a plan it
was! When Haman, one of the king's nobles, plotted to destroy
all the Jews in the kingdom, Mordecai persuaded Esther to inter-

vene on their behalf. "Who knows," he asked her, "but that you have come to royal position for such a time as this?"[1]

As I told Esther's story to the roomful of girls, I could see their interest growing with each twist of the plot. Most of them, I realized, had never heard the account before, and it wasn't long before they were sitting upright, worrying over Haman's evil plans, rooting for Esther, and cheering Mordecai on to victory. I laughed over their enthusiasm, and then reminded them of one of the story's central truths. "Esther was an ordinary girl," I said, "not much older and not very different from you. But God had a plan for her life, and he used her in a wonderful way—just like he can use each one of you."

Scripture is full of unlikely "heroes," ordinary people whom God used for extraordinary purposes when they looked past their own limitations and put their trust in him. Moses, for instance, had zero self-confidence when it came to public speaking, but God used him to repeatedly confront the most powerful king in the world and to deliver an entire nation from slavery. The prophet Jeremiah protested that he was only a child, but in God's hands he became the Lord's mouthpiece to Israel. And David was an unknown shepherd boy when God anointed him as Israel's future king.

These folks—and countless others—were regular people. But God knew their names even before they were born—just as he knows our names and the days of our lives even before they occur.[2] I love the way King David put it:

> For you created my inmost being;
> you knit me together in my mother's
> womb. . . .
> All the days ordained for me
> were written in your book
> before one of them came to be.[3]

Prayer Principle _____

> When you prayerfully entrust your "ordinary" children to the Lord, you invite him to use them in extraordinary ways.

_____ ❧

Your Job; God's Job

Susan Alexander Yates has five children, the youngest of whom is now in college. A best-selling author and speaker on family issues, Susan says that as she and her husband, John, have watched their children grow, they have tried to prepare them for whatever the future might hold. "Our job is to equip them," she says. "God's job is to call them."

In the Yates family, the equipping process runs the gamut from practicing fancy table manners ("you never know if God might call your children to dine with kings," Susan says) to working on a church mission in the inner city. Susan and John also study their kids' gifts, nourishing and pruning them in the event that these talents or abilities might be critical to God's plan for their future.

As parents, it is deceptively easy to confuse our job with God's and to start nudging our kids toward a particular career or ministry opportunity. Christian financial expert Ron Blue says that this is often true where family businesses are concerned, and that one of the most common mistakes business owners make is in assuming that they will pass their business on to their children—regardless of whether or not the kids are qualified to run it or are even interested in the job.

Rather than pigeonholing or manipulating our kids into a life path that might not line up with God's design, let's learn to see our kids through God's eyes—and align ourselves with his plan for their lives. To this end, author Jean Fleming recommends regular times of prayer and planning for each child. As we bring our children before the Lord, she says we should:

- *Acknowledge* God's hand on their lives, even before they were born.
- *Admit* any areas we resent in the way God put our children together.
- *Accept* God's design for each child, thanking him for how he or she is made.
- *Affirm* God's purpose in creating our children for his glory.
- *Ally* ourselves with God in his plans for their lives.[4]

Of course, trusting in God and his plan for our kids—along with accepting his timetable—is not always easy. But if we remember that he loves them (even more than we do), that he knows what is best for them (even more than we do), and that he promises to work in all things for the good of those who love him,[5] we can quit pushing and prodding—and get down to the real business of praying.

Prayer Principle _____

Asking God to fulfill his purposes in your children's lives involves aligning yourself with his plan.

Poised for Prayer

Thanks to a couple of prenatal angelic visits, both the Virgin Mary and her relative, Elizabeth, had some idea of who their sons would grow up to become and what they would do.[6] For the rest of us, though, taking hold of God's vision for our children can be daunting. One tactic that can help in this process is to prayerfully create a family mission statement.

A family mission statement is not unlike the purpose statements developed and used by many of today's successful corporations. It will reflect your family's values and goals, and it can make all the difference between a family life that is merely "good" or "acceptable" and one that is marked by excellence, fulfillment, and genuine joy.

Looking at Scripture, one theme running throughout the lives and circumstances of many of the Bible's characters is that God orchestrates events and works in people's hearts in order to *bring himself glory*. With this theme in mind, we have borrowed from Jeremiah 32:38–40 and Ephesians 3:20–21 in crafting the Berndt family mission, or purpose, statement:

> We are God's people, and he is our God.
> In all things we will strive to have singleness
> of heart and action,
> fearing God for our own good and
> for the good of our children's children.
> As God does immeasurably more than
> we could ever ask or imagine,
> we will give him the praise, the honor,
> and the glory for all generations.

As you shape your own purpose statement, think about the things that are most important to you, the goals you most want to accomplish. Your mission statement should reflect these values and priorities. And as your children grow, invite them to prayerfully design their own purpose statements—standards they can use to help them make wise choices as they confront life's decisions. For instance, if "developing a Christlike character" is part of your son's purpose statement, he may see playing on his high school soccer team as a way to foster godly attributes such as self-discipline, respect for authority, and a willingness to support and work with his peers. Joining the team may be costly in terms of time and energy, but if playing soccer lines up with his overall goals, he may decide it is well worth the effort.

As you pursue your family's mission, surround yourselves with people who share your vision. A subcategory to our family's purpose statement is that we want to support and encourage the teachers, staff members, and families represented in our children's schools. One of the things we have done to pursue this vision is to celebrate the beginning and ending of each school year by staging an informal ice-cream party with our friends, the Keshians. We make our own sundaes, play games in the backyard, flop on the ground and look up at the stars, and then pray together for our kids and their school.

In addition to encouraging us as parents, these informal prayer times are a terrific way to show our children how to integrate their faith into their daily lives. The kids may have no idea that our get-togethers are working to fulfill God's purpose for our families. But as they see God's hand on their classmates, their teachers, and their school, they cannot help but sense that, through prayer, they have played a part in his master plan.

～ Prayers You Can Use ～

Heavenly Father...

You know the plans you have for _____, plans to prosper him and not to harm him, plans to give him hope and a future. Cause _____ to call upon you and come and pray to you, and then listen to him, O Lord. Let him seek you with all his heart, and find you when he does seek you. (Jeremiah 29:11–13)

～

Fulfill every good purpose in _____'s life and every act prompted by her faith, so that the name of our Lord Jesus Christ may be glorified in her life. (2 Thessalonians 1:11–12)

～

Let _____ be careful and wise in how he lives, making the most of every opportunity and understanding your will for his life. (Ephesians 5:15–17)

～

Work in _____ so she will think and act according to your good purpose. (Philippians 2:13)

∾

Fulfill your purpose for _____ *; do not abandon the works of your hands. (Psalm 138:8)*

∾

Thank you that no eye has seen, no ear has heard, no mind has conceived what you have prepared for _____ *because he loves you. Cause him to be willing to wait on you, and act on his behalf. (1 Corinthians 2:9; Isaiah 64:4)*

∾

Thank you for beginning a good work in _____, *and that you will carry it on to completion until the day of Christ Jesus. (Philippians 1:6)*

∾

Let _____ *be glad for all you are planning for her. Let her be patient in trouble, and prayerful always. (Romans 12:12 LB)*

∾

No matter what _____ *is planning in his heart, let your purpose prevail in his life. (Proverbs 19:21)*

CHAPTER EIGHTEEN

PRAYING FOR YOUR CHILD'S MARRIAGE

He who finds a wife finds what is good
and receives favor from the LORD.

— Proverbs 18:22

"HOW DID YOU KNOW ROBBIE WAS THE ONE FOR YOU?"

Anne's question caught me off guard. Her daughter, Heather, had developed a special relationship with a young man, and it was no secret that the whole family hoped he might be "The One." When she heard her mother's question, Heather looked up from the book she was reading and waited for my answer.

"I don't know," I said. "I just knew. He asked me to marry him—and I said yes."

I could tell my answer didn't satisfy them. I wished I could have said that God had spoken to me, that he had given me a sign, or that I had fasted and prayed for wisdom—anything that sounded better than "I don't know; I just said yes."

Truth be told, I had been praying for my husband—whoever he might be—for years. As a teenager, I had accompanied my folks to a Bill Gothard seminar ("Institute in Basic Youth Conflicts") and come away with a fairly clear vision of what made for a good marriage. That I wanted a Christian husband was a given. On top of that, I wanted him to have qualities that included a clear conscience, a sense of purpose, a willingness to respect and yield to authority, and the ability to earn a living. And as I prayed for my future husband, I also asked God to protect him, to help him to do well in school, and to give him a strong and loving relationship with his parents.

When I met Robbie in college, it never occurred to me that he might be the answer to my prayers. For one thing, he was not a Christian. He had a church background, but he had never heard about having a personal relationship with Jesus Christ—and he didn't seem overly eager to go down that road. But he was handsome, athletic, smart, and fun—and so, figuring that he would be a great catch for *somebody,* I introduced him to one of my sorority sisters.

But God had other ideas. To make a long story short, Robbie wound up giving his life to Christ, and our friendship blossomed into a full-fledged romance. But we didn't talk much about the future, so I was somewhat surprised when, just three weeks after graduation, he asked me to marry him. As it turned out, I was the only one taken by surprise. Robbie's folks were in on his plan, and he had already asked for—and received—my parents' blessing.

I said yes—but years later, when Anne asked me *how* I knew Robbie was the one, I began to wonder. How *had* I known what to say? Caught by surprise by his proposal, how could I have accepted it with such confidence and peace?

I didn't know—and I might never have known, had I not started working on this chapter. I surveyed several mature Christians (including my parents) and asked them to tell me about their prayers for their children's eventual marriages.

"Well," my father said, "from the time you were a teenager, we prayed a two-part prayer. First, we asked God to put a hedge around your emotions and not permit you to be drawn to anyone he didn't want you to be with. And second, we asked that when the Lord sent the one he had chosen, that the Holy Spirit would rule in your heart. We prayed that the peace of Christ would rule in your heart—sort of like an umpire in your decision."

I wanted to laugh out loud. My parents' prayer—taken straight out of Colossians 3:15—was the reason I said yes! I couldn't wait to call Anne and revise my answer to her question: "I knew that Robbie was the one for me because my parents had spent years praying for my decision. The peace I felt was a direct answer to a specific prayer!"

Prayer Principle _____

It's never too early to start praying for your children's choice of a marriage partner, for their eventual spouse, and for their marriage itself.

When God Throws You a Curveball

Marjorie and her husband, Dan, were delighted when their son, Dan Jr., announced his desire to marry his girlfriend, Sarah. Sarah was from a strong Christian home—and it showed: She was as beautiful in spirit as she was in appearance, and Dan Jr. had courted her with the blessing of both of their families. Marjorie recalled the many nights she had spent rocking little Dan in her arms, praying for his choice of a marriage partner. In Sarah, her dreams had come true.

Marjorie couldn't say as much for her other daughter-in-law. When their son, David, had declared his plans to marry Taylor, Marjorie and Dan had been stunned. David had only known Taylor for two months—and Marjorie and Dan had never even met the girl! Surprised as they were by David's news, it was nothing compared to the shock wave they felt a month later when David announced—on Father's Day—that he had *already* been married for two weeks!

Marjorie and Dan knew they had a decision to make. They could welcome Taylor into their family, or they could reject her. From a strictly emotional standpoint, the latter course seemed the better option. Marjorie and Dan had prayed that David's wife would come from a godly home with parents who were committed to each other and to Jesus Christ. Taylor, they suspected, was a far cry from this standard.

In her heart, though, Marjorie knew what she and Dan had to do. They arranged to meet David and Taylor at a restaurant, where they planned to sweep their feelings aside and extend a warm welcome to their new daughter-in-law, blessing her marriage to their son. David had not been known to make the wisest of choices . . . but how bad could his new wife really be?

Had Marjorie and Dan known the truth, they might have thought twice before arranging the meeting. Taylor, it turned out, was the product of a broken marriage, with parents who had each been married four or five times. Her mother, a prescription drug addict, was living with one of a string of men she had dated since Taylor had run away from home at age fifteen. Taylor had never finished high school, and as she stared across the table at her new in-laws after filling them in on her life, the challenge was obvious. "Now," she said, leaning forward on her elbows, "do you still want to bless me?"

Marjorie found her emotions to be in a whirl. *Help me, Lord!* she inwardly cried. *I can't love this girl! I'm not even sure I can love my own son. But I am willing, if you'll show me how. I don't feel like loving them ... but I know you want me to, and I will obey you.*

It seemed like an impossibly insignificant step, but once Marjorie and Dan purposed to love Taylor and accept the marriage, God began to reveal the working of his hand. For years, David had carried a chip on his shoulder, rebelling against his parents in ways that his three siblings had never dreamed of doing. Through it all, Marjorie had continued to pray for him, dropping (as she puts it) "pennies through the slot" and trusting God to guide and protect him.

For the most part, Marjorie saw little evidence that God had even heard her prayers, but now, with his marriage to Taylor, David seemed to change almost overnight. "God," Marjorie observed, "used the unlikely scenario of David's marriage to catapult our son into a responsibility, sensitivity, and maturity from which he had fled for years.

"And," she added, "I truly love Taylor. She is perfect for David—and she has become our fifth child."

Unbelievable as it seemed, Taylor—with all the baggage she carried with her—was God's answer to a parent's loving prayers. Had Marjorie and Dan failed to love and accept her, they would have missed out on one of God's richest blessings.

Prayer Principle _____

> When you pray for your child's marriage, God will hear and answer you. You can trust in his answer—even when it looks like there's been some kind of mistake!

Be Specific

As we think about stories like Marjorie's, some of us might be tempted to rekindle the practice of "arranged" marriages. Thanks to the privilege of prayer, however, we can take advantage of an even better opportunity. We can ask God to choose our kids' spouses—and, through prayer, we can begin influencing and blessing our in-laws' lives long before we ever meet them.

Rather than fingering a particular *person* for our children to marry, it would be wise for us to pray for particular *character traits* or *attributes* in the spouse God has in mind. When the time came for Isaac to marry, Abraham had some fairly concrete ideas about the type of wife he wanted for his son.

She couldn't be a Canaanite; rather, he wanted someone from his own country, someone whose family acknowledged the Lord. Too old to make the journey himself, Abraham sent his chief servant to find a wife for his boy.

As the servant approached Abraham's hometown, he prayed a very specific prayer: "O LORD, . . . I am standing beside this spring, and the daughters of the townspeople are coming out to draw water. May it be that when I say to a girl, 'Please let down your jar that I may have a drink,' and she says, 'Drink, and I'll water your camels too'—let her be the one you have chosen for your servant Isaac. By this I will know that you have shown kindness to my master."[1]

Obviously, Abraham's servant was asking God for a sign. But I think there was more to his prayer than this. I think that when he prayed for a girl who would offer him water—and water his camels too (not an easy job, by any means!)—the servant was asking God to show him a girl with the kindness, thoughtfulness, generosity, patience, and strength that Isaac would value in a wife. And indeed, Rebekah turned out to be all of these things, and more.

As you pray for your children's eventual mates, keep James 4:2 in mind ("You do not have, because you do not ask God"), and be specific. One of my friends—whose own parents are divorced—prays that her children will marry men and women from unbroken homes. Another friend has asked God to let her kids find their mates early in life, both so they can enjoy the blessing of marriage and to lessen the pressures of sexual temptation during their adult years. Two young men we know are praying for wives whose lives are marked by honesty, virtue, purity, and a good sense of humor. And one girl told me she wants a husband with thin lips!

Is it wrong to be this specific with God? I don't think so—particularly when our requests are wrapped in an overarching desire to see God's will be done. In fact, I think God *loves* to answer these prayers: As Matthew 7:11 puts it, "If you, then, though you are evil, know how to give good gifts to your children, how much more will your Father in heaven give good gifts to those who ask him!"

Prayer Principle _____

> When you pray for your child's mate,
> don't be afraid to be specific!

Poised for Prayer

What are *your* desires for your children's marriages? One of my prayers is that my kids will marry people who love God with all their heart, soul, mind, and strength, and who will love their neighbors as themselves, as described in Mark 12:29–31. Another is that my children and their spouses will know the blessings and joy that go with honoring their parents, according to Exodus 20:12.

Keep a list of your prayers, complete with dates and Scripture references, so you'll have a record of God's faithfulness when he answers them. Also, as you pray for your children's marriages, don't forget to pray for your kids themselves, asking God to shape them into godly young men and women. Authors Ned and Drew Ryun point to the value in the years before marriage, saying that this is the time when "character is developed, skills learned, and the flesh and its desires mastered. It is a time for serving the Lord with an undivided heart—before the demands of marriage and family begin to vie for one's attention and time."[2] Let me suggest two Scripture passages that make wonderful "marriage-prep" prayers. Insert your children's names into these verses, asking God to make your children, as the old *Fiddler on the Roof* song puts it, "good husbands and wives."

Proverbs 31: A Prayer for a Godly Woman

_____ *is worth far more than rubies. Her husband has full confidence in her and lacks nothing of value. She brings him good, not harm, all the days of her life.... She sets about her work vigorously; her arms are strong for her tasks....* _____ *opens her arms to the poor and extends her hands to the needy.... She is clothed with strength and dignity; she can laugh at the days to come. She speaks with wisdom, and faithful instruction is on her tongue.* _____ *watches over the affairs of her household and does not eat the bread of idleness. Her children arise and call her blessed; her husband also, and he praises her: Many women do noble things, but you,* _____, *surpass them all. Charm is deceptive and beauty fleeting; but a woman who fears the Lord is to be praised.*

Psalm 112: A Prayer for a Godly Man

Blessed is _____ *who fears the Lord, who finds great delight in his commands. His children will be mighty in the land; the generation of the upright will be blessed. Wealth and riches are in his house, and his righteousness endures* forever. Even in darkness light dawns for _____, for the gracious and compassionate and righteous man. Good will come to him who is generous and lends freely, who conducts his affairs with justice. Surely _____ will never be shaken; a righteous man will be remembered forever. He will have no fear of bad news; his heart is steadfast, trusting in the Lord. His heart is secure, he will have no fear; in the end he will look in triumph on his foes. _____ has scattered abroad his gifts to the poor, his righteousness endures forever; his horn will be lifted high in honor.

Prayers You Can Use

Heavenly Father...

*D*o not allow _____ to be yoked together with an unbelieving girlfriend or spouse. For what do righteousness and wickedness have in common? Or what fellowship can light have with darkness? Rather, let him be drawn to a woman who calls you God, who is counted among your people. (2 Corinthians 6:14–17)

∾

*C*ause _____ to be willing to wait for your perfect timing in finding a husband, even as Jacob waited seven years to marry his beloved Rachel. And, as you did for Jacob, let the waiting period seem to go by quickly. (Genesis 29:20)

∾

223

*L*et _____ be a considerate husband who treats his wife with respect, so that nothing will hinder his prayers. Let him love his wife in the same way that Christ loved the church, being willing to give himself up for her. (1 Peter 3:7; Ephesians 5:25)

∽

*L*et _____ be a wife who is worthy of respect, not a malicious talker but temperate and trustworthy in everything. Let her be willing to submit to her husband as to the Lord. (1 Timothy 3:11; Ephesians 5:22)

∽

*C*ause _____ to honor marriage, and to keep his marriage bed pure, knowing that you will judge the adulterer and the sexually immoral. (Hebrews 13:4)

∽

*L*et _____ and her future spouse flee from sexual immorality, recognizing that their bodies are temples of the Holy Spirit. Let them know that they belong to you, and cause them to honor you with their bodies. (1 Corinthians 6:18–20)

∽

*B*less _____'s marriage, Lord. As he grows older, let him continue to rejoice in the wife of his youth. (Proverbs 5:18)

∾

*S*how _____ and her husband how to love each other deeply, for love covers over a multitude of sins. Let them make every effort to do what leads to peace and to mutual edification. (1 Peter 4:8; Romans 14:19)

∾

*P*rotect _____ from divorce or marital strife. What you have joined together in _____'s marriage, let man not separate. (Mark 10:9)

∾

*J*ust as _____ received Christ Jesus as Lord, let him continue to live in him. Let _____'s marriage relationship be rooted and built up in Jesus, strengthened in the faith, and overflowing with thankfulness. (Colossians 2:6–7)

CHAPTER NINETEEN

PRAYING FOR YOUR CHILD'S MANAGEMENT OF TIME AND MONEY

Now it is required that those who have been
given a trust must prove faithful.

— 1 Corinthians 4:2

"GUESS WHAT, MOM?" FIVE-YEAR-OLD HOUSTON ASKED HIS mother. "They're selling candy at Vacation Bible School this week! Can we buy some?"

Margaret smiled. Houston loved candy as much as the next kid, but she knew his enthusiasm had deeper roots: If the children could raise enough money through the candy sale, their VBS leaders had promised that the proceeds would be used to send five children in the Dominican Republic to a mission school. A budding entrepreneur, Houston was already mapping out his sales territory. "Maybe we could sell candy to the people at Daddy's office," he suggested.

As the week wore on, Houston and the other children began to look forward to the daily announcement letting them know how far they had to go to reach their goal. Excitement was running high. The money, however, came in at a more sluggish pace, and by Thursday it became apparent to everyone that, unless something incredible happened, they would fall short of their goal.

Thursday night Houston sat on his bed, eyeing his shiny yellow piggy bank. He lifted it, enjoying its heavy weight in his hands and the sound the coins made as they shifted together. He had saved long and hard, carefully dropping his pennies, nickels, dimes, and quarters through the slot. What should he do with all that money?

"Mom?" Houston called out suddenly. "Do you have a baggie I can put my money in?"

As Margaret rooted around for a plastic bag, Houston explained his decision. "I want to give my money to help the children in the Dominican Republic go to a good school. I will take it to Vacation Bible School tomorrow."

Touched by her son's willingness to share what he had with people he didn't even know, Margaret held back her tears. "Houston," she said gently, "I think that is a fine idea. When we give our best to God, it makes him smile. And when we are generous toward others, we can always trust that God will take care of us."

The next day, Margaret stood in the back of the room, watching as the children heard the news: Not only had they reached their goal, but they had brought in so much money that day that they would be able to send *ten* children to the mission school. As one, the kids leaped out of their seats and

227

cheered. Houston, Margaret observed, was grinning from ear to ear. He knew he had been part of a miracle.

But the best part was yet to come. That afternoon, while the fund-raising triumph was still fresh in Houston's mind, Margaret's neighbor came to the door. "Oh, Houston," she said, "I forgot to pay you for feeding my dog a few weeks ago. Here's the money I owe you—I'm so sorry it's late."

Margaret and Houston stared in amazement at the cash the woman offered. It was more than twice the amount that Houston had given away that morning!

This time Margaret couldn't help but cry. Not only had her son experienced the joy of *giving*, but in one amazing moment he had learned the joy of *receiving* from his loving and faithful heavenly Father. God was so good!

"Hey, Mom," Houston said, interrupting her thoughts. "You were right. God always takes care of us, doesn't he?"

Prayer Principle _____

> Praying for your children's ability to manage money involves praying that they will trust God as the supplier of all their needs.

More Is Caught Than Taught

The Bible contains more than 2,300 references to money and possessions, and Jesus talked about money and money management more than any other single issue, weaving financial principles into everyday situations. "See that poor widow over there?" he would say, directing his disciples' gaze toward a woman who had quietly dropped two small coins into the temple treasury. "She has put in more than everyone else. All the others gave gifts out of their wealth; but she gave her all—everything she had to live on."[1]

Our friends, Judy and Ron Blue, have spent more than thirty years studying Jesus' teachings on financial management. And like Jesus, they have worked to communicate these principles to countless others—Ron through his work as the managing partner of one of America's leading financial and investment planning firms, and Judy via the many Bible studies and discipleship groups she leads for other women. They are popular speakers and best-selling authors, but what I find especially intriguing about their message is how they have managed to explain the principles to each of their five children.

Every year, Ron and Judy go away on a planning weekend to talk and pray about everything from their family vacations to their kids' education. On the theory that their resources ultimately belong to God and that every spending decision is, therefore, a spiritual decision, they ask God for wisdom regarding things like budgeting, financial goal-setting, and investing. They also pray that their kids will understand and apply God's principles for money management.

When their children were young, Ron and Judy worked to convey these principles in practical ways, using tools like the envelope system to teach simple budgeting concepts. Once a month they would give each child a specific amount of cash, divided among five envelopes: Tithe, Save, Spend, Gifts, and

Clothes. The kids quickly learned the reality of limited resources, the value in delaying gratification, and the freedom that comes from allocating your money according to a predetermined plan.

"One day," Judy told me several years ago, "our children will be somebody's spouse, somebody's employee, somebody's parent, somebody's boss. When we teach them how to manage their money, we are equipping them with the skills they'll need throughout their lives, no matter what sort of job they have or what kind of income they earn."

Already this equipping process has proved its worth: Ron and Judy's daughters used principles learned via the envelope system to plan their weddings, and their husbands are grateful for the wisdom and resourcefulness they have brought to their marriages. And, thanks to the lessons they have learned about saving, investing, and trusting in God's provision, each of Ron and Judy's kids has felt free to make career decisions based on his or her dreams and goals rather than on a worldly desire to "get rich quick."

The envelope system was just one of many teaching tools Ron and Judy used as their children grew up. But from my perspective as an outsider to their family, it seemed that the greatest lessons didn't come from envelopes, charts, or other money management techniques. Rather, I think the best teaching tool was the way in which Ron and Judy consistently demonstrated wise stewardship for their kids, acknowledging God as their provider and looking to him to help them allocate their financial resources. Quietly and steadily, they modeled their message—and this example, coupled with their heartfelt prayers, served as the most powerful teacher of all.

Prayer Principle _____

Praying for your children's management of time and money includes asking God to help you model biblical stewardship so that your kids can see how God's principles work.

Stewardship of Time and Talents

Wise financial stewardship depends on knowing and using biblical, time-tested principles to manage the material assets God gives us. In the same way, these principles can be used to help our children handle their other God-given resources, including things like time and talents.

Our older girls were barely out of diapers the first time our friends Jim and Anne called to ask whether we wanted their teenage daughter, Catharine, to be our nanny for a few weeks. Not knowing how much this service would cost, we were uncertain as to how to respond, but Jim and Anne were quick to dismiss our concerns. It wasn't about money, they said. Catharine was being homeschooled, and serving as our nanny would help sharpen her skills and talents, as well as her gift of service.

Not that these things needed much sharpening! Catharine had only been in our home for a couple of days before we realized that she had a genuine gift for child rearing. Almost instinctively, she knew when to slather the kids with affection and when to present a firmer face, and as she lovingly cared for the girls, I found myself learning from her example. Not a moment was wasted. When Catharine wasn't mopping the kitchen floor, she was reading Bible stories and other books to the children; when she wasn't changing a diaper, she was experimenting with a new recipe for our dinner.

I felt incredibly selfish, soaking up the energy of a hard-working girl half my age. But Catharine truly seemed to thrive on what she was doing. She regarded her education as more than just academics, and the chance to learn how to manage a household was simply one of many skills she wanted to learn—including everything from raising sheep to speaking German!

Catharine saw her time and talents as gifts from God, resources she could use for his kingdom. And after two weeks of watching her in action, I began to pray that my children would one day share her industrious spirit, her passionate commitment to serving others, and her skillful ability to use and manage her gifts.

Romans 14:12 says that all of us will one day stand before God and give an account of ourselves. When God looks at Catharine and the way she managed her money, her time, and her talents, I know what he will say. He'll say the same thing he said to the faithful money managers in Matthew 25:23: "Well done, good and faithful servant! You have been faithful with a few things; I will put you in charge of many things. Come and share your master's happiness!"

Can you think of a more exciting reward for your own children?

Prayer Principle _____

Praying for your children's management of time, talents, and money can open the door for them to enjoy God's rewards—both now and throughout eternity.

Poised for Prayer

As you teach your kids how to handle their time and money, think of putting coins into a piggy bank. The more teaching (and prayer) you deposit now, the bigger the payoff will be down the road. Scripture offers countless principles and lessons you can draw on, but if you want some help getting started, here are three of my favorite "time and money management" prayer pointers, gleaned from Ron Blue's books (see the recommended reading list at the end of this book):

1. *God owns it all.* As Psalm 24:1 says, "The earth is the LORD's, and everything in it." Pray that your children will recognize God's ownership of their resources, and that when they consider spending time or money on something, their main question won't be "Can I afford it?" but "Would God want me to use his time or money in this way?"

2. *There will always be unlimited ways to allocate limited resources.* It doesn't matter whether you are five

years old or fifty, or whether you have five dollars to spend or fifty thousand—your spending options will always exceed the money (or time) you have. Pray that your children will have the wisdom to order their priorities, and that they will learn to delay gratification so that they are not tempted to cheat, steal, or fall prey to discontent when they cannot have everything they want.

3. *Generosity is the key to freedom.* Matthew 6:24 says, "You cannot serve both God and Money." Pray that your children will serve God wholeheartedly, and that they will never be enslaved by financial fear or greed. Pray that they will hold their wealth—their time, their money, their talents—with an open hand and a generous heart, looking for opportunities to share their blessings with others.

Prayers You Can Use

Heavenly Father...

Teach _____ to sow generously, that she might also reap generously. Let her giving be marked by cheerfulness rather than by reluctance, and supply all her needs so that she will abound in every good work. (2 Corinthians 9:6–8)

Let _____ acknowledge your ownership of his resources, knowing that everything he has comes from your hand. Let _____ always look to you to meet all his needs, according to your glorious riches in Christ Jesus. (1 Chronicles 29:14; Philippians 4:19)

∾

Cause _____ to put her trust in you, O Lord; let her say, "You are my God. My times and my days are in your hands." (Psalm 31:14–15)

∾

Enable _____ to support and provide for his relatives, especially his immediate family, so that no one can accuse him of denying his faith or behaving worse than an unbeliever would. (1 Timothy 5:8)

∾

Give _____ a grateful heart, and equip her to rejoice, to pray, and to give thanks in all circumstances. (1 Thessalonians 5:16–18)

∾

Keep _____'s life free from the love of money and let him be content with what he has, knowing that you, O Lord, will never leave him or forsake him. Let him be like Paul, who knew how to be content in any and every situation, *whether well fed or hungry, whether living in plenty or in want. (Hebrews 13:5; Philippians 4:12)*

∾

Help _____ understand that "he who gathers money little by little makes it grow." Don't let _____ wear herself out to get rich; give her the wisdom she needs to show restraint. (Proverbs 13:11; 23:4)

∾

Teach _____ to number his days and recognize how few they are; help him to spend them as he should. (Psalm 90:12 LB)

∾

Cause _____ to look carefully how she walks, not as unwise but as wise, making the most of her time and understanding your will. (Ephesians 5:15–17 RSV)

∾

Don't let _____ be arrogant or put his hope in wealth, which is so uncertain, but let him put his hope in you. Let him enjoy all that you have provided for him, and cause him to be rich in good deeds, being generous and always willing to share. Let _____ lay up treasure for himself as a firm foundation for the coming age, so that he can take hold of the life that is truly life. (1 Timothy 6:17–19)

∾

I pray that _____ would be trustworthy in how she handles wealth, and that she would be single-minded in her devotion to you, recognizing that she cannot serve both God and Money. (Luke 16:10–13)

CHAPTER TWENTY

PRAYING FOR YOUR CHILD WHEN HE OR SHE LEAVES YOUR NEST

Be strong and courageous. Do not be terrified;
do not be discouraged, for the LORD your God will be
with you wherever you go.

—Joshua 1:9

"PLEASE REMEMBER TO PRAY FOR JENNIFER," DAD SAID, AS OUR telephone conversation drew to a close. "She's not feeling at all well—I think she's got some kind of flu bug. Mom and I have put her at the top of our prayer list."

The flu was the last thing my sister Jen needed. A high school science teacher, she was already sagging under piles of ungraded papers, lesson plans, and discipline problems with her students. She never complained—in fact, she seemed to truly enjoy both the work and the kids—but I knew she couldn't afford to get sick.

"I will pray for her," I agreed. "And little Robbie could use your prayers, too. Last night he tried to dive off Hillary's back onto his bed, and he slit his cheek open from his temple to his lip."

"Ouch," Dad said. "Didn't he just gash his nose the same way?"

"Yes. But that scar is starting to heal. And Dad," I said, "please keep praying for the book—it's due in less than a month. And don't forget: Our house goes on the market next week, and Robbie will be out of town on business, and we're supposed to go to Williamsburg with his parents this weekend, but the baby-sitter just called and she's got bronchitis, so I've got to find somebody else to keep the kids."

"Hey!" Dad laughed. "Are you trying to bump Jennifer out of the top spot?"

"I'm working on it!" I replied, knowing full well that there was room for all of us on our parents' prayer docket.

Years ago I worked as a television producer, and I remember doing a show on adult children of alcoholics, the gist of which was that the problems and issues surrounding a parent's alcoholism tend to follow children into adulthood, even when they no longer live with their folks. I think the same thing happens with adult children of praying parents, only instead of problems following you around, you have God's blessings, protection, and love.

My parents, Claire and Allen Rundle, are true prayer warriors, especially when it comes to their children. They don't live near any of their kids—and at various points in their adult lives, my siblings have lived in China, Africa, Russia, and Switzerland—but the geographic separation has only served to strengthen our family ties. Mom and Dad act as our "Command Center," fielding prayer requests and keeping updated on our lives via e-mail messages and telephone calls, and then they pass the news around the family, calling to remind us to "pour on the prayer" whenever anyone has an important meeting, a special date, or a sick child.

Because of the example set by my folks—and because of the many ways I have seen God answer their prayers—I have no fear for my own children's future. In fact, I look forward to praying for them when they go off to college, when they choose a career, and when they get married. And I am especially eager to use what I've learned about God's promises and his faithfulness in order to be able to pray for my grandchildren like my parents do, capitalizing on verses like Psalm 100:5—"For the LORD is good and his love endures forever; his faithfulness continues through all generations."

Prayer Principle _____

> For adult children of praying parents, prayer gives God an invitation to pour out his blessings, protection, and love— proving his faithfulness to all generations.

_____

Power in God's Presence

Does the fact that I do not fear for my children's future mean that I expect everything to go smoothly for them, or that

I think they will always enjoy health, happiness, and freedom from trouble or financial need? Not at all. In fact, looking again at my parents' example, they seem to have spent more than their fair share of time "in the trenches," prayerfully carrying my siblings and me through broken relationships, difficult career choices, and even life-threatening circumstances.

As a high school senior, Jennifer was diagnosed with colon cancer, a disease that rarely occurs in young people. Doctors held out slim hopes for her recovery—in fact, according to one study they later shared with our family, there were no survivors among children and teens with the disease. Yet Jen and my folks clung to verses such as Ephesians 3:20–21: "Now to him who is able to do immeasurably more than all we ask or imagine, according to his power that is at work within us, to him be glory in the church and in Christ Jesus throughout all generations, for ever and ever!" And God *did* do more than any of us could have asked or imagined: In addition to giving Jennifer a miraculous healing, he used her story to touch and transform countless lives.[1]

Likewise, my sister Mary has found herself in some rather unsettling situations. As a college student, she opted to spend a semester studying in China, where she often traveled alone in remote areas. More recently, her job as an international trade lawyer has taken her to some of the world's hottest spots, where she has worked under the threat (and occasional reality) of terrorism, political upheaval, and citywide rioting.

Do these dangers cause my parents to worry? I thought they might—after all, they are only human—but Mom set me straight. "While Mary was in China," she said, "we poured on the prayer for her, but we never worried. In fact, it was only after she came home [which, incidentally, was just a few months before the Tiananmen Square massacre in 1989] that we realized how fervent our prayers had been. It's like when you are sick, and you don't realize how bad it is until you get well again. Only then do you know what you have been through."

I believe that what sustained my parents when Mary was alone in China or when Jen was battling cancer was an awareness of God's presence and his hand on each of their lives. I can't help but think that Moses' mother must have had a similar sense of God's nearness when she placed her infant son in a basket and set him adrift on the crocodile-infested Nile River. And sure enough, the Lord protected the baby, bringing him into Pharaoh's own household to be raised among the sons of Egypt.

Later, when God revealed his presence to Moses in the form of a burning bush and commanded him to deliver the Israelites from Egyptian bondage, Moses balked. "Who am I," he protested, "that I should go to Pharaoh and bring the Israelites out of Egypt?" God's answer to Moses is, I think, one of the best lines in the Bible. He doesn't tell Moses what to say to Pharaoh or how to approach him; rather, he simply says, "I will be with you."[2] And really, what more could Moses want? What more could any of us want than to know that God Almighty, the Creator and Lord of the universe, is with us? What more could we want for our children?

"Moses knew it was God's presence in Israel that set the people apart from all other nations," writes evangelist David Wilkerson. "And the same is true of the church of Jesus Christ today. The only thing that sets us apart from nonbelievers is

God's being 'with us'—leading us, guiding us, working his will in and through us."[3]

If I could pray just one prayer for my kids, this is what it would be: *Go with my children, Lord. Be with them wherever they go, and in whatever they do.* I would pray that they would know Jesus as their *Immanuel*—literally, "God with us." I would appropriate the promise that God made to Joshua when Joshua succeeded Moses as Israel's leader: "Be strong and courageous. Do not be terrified; do not be discouraged, for the LORD your God will be with you wherever you go."[4]

Prayer Principle

> Although the future is uncertain, through prayer you can entrust your children's lives to a sovereign and dependable God whose love for them is never in doubt—a God who promises to be with them wherever they go.

Building Altars

My brother, David, recently graduated from the University of Virginia, where the commencement ceremonies always include a grand procession down Thomas Jefferson's lawn. It is an event steeped in history and tradition, a walk made familiar by generations of graduates. David was walking with a group of his friends when he spotted our parents in the crowd of onlookers. Removing himself from his peers, he threaded his way through the procession and ran over to our folks, encircling Dad's neck and planting a kiss on his cheek in a very public display of gratitude and affection.

A few days later I received a letter from Dad describing David's impromptu embrace and telling me how much it had meant to him as a father. Dad went on to recount about a dozen similar memories and blessings from the years his children had spent in college, pointing out that they were "all a testimony of God's tender mercies, one after another after another, being bestowed upon our family."

Dad wrapped up his letter with a challenge: "God is so faithful," he wrote, "and we must remember to stop occasionally and 'build an altar of thanksgiving' before we hurry on our way."

The Bible is bursting with altars built by those who wanted a lasting memorial of God's faithfulness, his promises, and his life-changing power. Noah built one after the great flood; Jacob built one after his conversion experience; Moses built one after God took the Israelites safely through the Red Sea.[5] In each of these instances—and in numerous others—the altar signified the time and place where God showed up and proved his love.

Prayer Principle _____

The altars you build with praise and thanksgiving
are the pillars of a vibrant prayer life.

Poised for Prayer

Do you have altars in your own life—places or situations in which you know God intervened on your behalf or provided an answer to your prayers? When a need arises, do you focus on God's faithfulness and his power—or are you consumed by the problem at hand?

We've covered a number of prayer topics in this book, but there are undoubtedly many other issues and concerns that can join forces to assault your trust in God. The Bible tells us not to worry about anything. "Instead," Paul writes, "pray about everything; tell God your needs and don't forget to thank him for his answers."[6]

If you haven't done so already, take some time to reflect on the ways God has blessed your family. Write these blessings down, building your own "altar" of thanksgiving and remembrance. Share this testimony with your children, and encourage them to erect their own altars as God works in their lives. In this way, when your children leave your nest, both you and they will have a tangible record of God's faithfulness and his love.

Your altar might be a basket containing slips of paper on which you have recorded God's answers or his guidance. It might be a specific time and place each week or month when your family gets together to pray and reflect on God's goodness. It might be something as simple as a prayer journal in which you write down your prayers, the promises from the Bible, and his answers to your prayers.

No matter what form your altar takes, be sure to refer to it often as a means of building your faith, keeping your relationship with God on track, and filling you with a peace that is rooted in the certain knowledge that God Almighty is in control—and that he is worthy of your trust, your praise, and your gratitude.

∽ Prayers You Can Use ∽

Heavenly Father...

*E*nable _____ to be strong and courageous. Don't let him get frightened or discouraged, but let him know that you will be with him wherever he goes. (Joshua 1:9)

∽

*B*e _____ 's Lord and God. Teach her what is best for her, and direct her in the way she should go. (Isaiah 48:17)

∽

*H*elp us to train _____ in the way that he should go, so that when he is old he will not turn from it. (Proverbs 22:6)

∽

*C*ause _____ to delight in you, and give her the desires of her heart. Let her commit her way to you, trusting in you as you make her righteousness shine like the dawn. (Psalm 37:4–5)

❧

Do immeasurably more in _____'s life than all we could ever ask or imagine, according to your power that is at work within him. Glorify yourself through his life, and for generations to come. (Ephesians 3:20–21)

❧

Teach _____, O Lord, to follow your decrees. Give her understanding to keep your law and obey it with all her heart. Direct _____ in the path of your commands, and let her find delight there. Turn her heart toward your statutes and not toward selfish gain. (Psalm 119:33–36)

❧

Let _____ trust in you with all his heart and lean not on his own understanding. In all his ways and in everything he does, let him acknowledge your lordship and your presence, and direct his paths in his career, his marriage, his ministry, and in his walk with you. (Proverbs 3:5–6)

❧

Let _____ praise you with all her heart and soul and never forget your benefits. Forgive her sins, heal her diseases, redeem her life, and crown her with love and compassion. Satisfy her desires with good things. Let _____ know that from everlasting to everlasting, your love is with those who fear you, and your righteousness will be with her children's children as they keep your commandments and remember to obey your precepts. *(Psalm 103:1–5, 17–18)*

∾

We have prayed for _____, and you have granted us what we have asked. So now we give him to you, Lord. For his whole life he will be given over to the Lord. (1 Samuel 1:27–28)

∾

Throughout _____'s life, let her continue to grow as Jesus did—in wisdom and stature, and in favor with you and with other people. (Luke 2:52)

THE LIFE-CHANGING WORK OF PRAYER

Let us run with perseverance the race marked out for us. Let us
fix our eyes on Jesus, the author and perfecter of our faith.

—Hebrews 12:1–2

THROUGHOUT THIS BOOK WE'VE SEEN HOW GOD MOVES IN ANSWER
to believing prayer. Sometimes his answers have come quickly;
more often, they have unfolded after days, weeks, or even years
of intercession.

"*Why does it have to be this way?*" I found myself wondering—complaining—aloud to God one day as I ran along
the beach. "*I know you want what's best for our family. Why
don't you just go ahead and answer my prayers the first time
I ask? Why does prayer have to be such hard work?*"

In retrospect, I can think of several possible answers to
these questions; many of the answers are in fact covered by

author Dutch Sheets in his book titled *Intercessory Prayer* (see the recommended reading list). But none of those answers is what came to my mind that day on the beach. Instead, God reminded me of my longing to see my children "grow up" spiritually and intellectually. As our older girls approach their teenage years, I want them to make wise, responsible choices—without relying on me as the stage manager for their lives.

It would be much easier—and often a lot less messy—for me to continue treating Hillary and Annesley the way I did when they were younger: choosing their playmates, directing their leisure time, screening virtually all that they read or saw, and reviewing every last page of their homework to ensure that it was done properly. But I know that the growth process involves letting them make choices and do things for themselves—even when it means they have to work, sweat, and sometimes even cry.

I think prayer can be a lot like that. It would be *much* easier—and always less messy—if God simply took charge, directing our prayers like laser beams and then answering them on the spot. But while such an approach might ensure that God's will would be done, it would do nothing for our own spiritual growth, our character, or our ongoing relationship with the Lord.

Just as I want my own children to change and mature, so God wants us—his children—to "grow up" in our faith—and the work of prayer is one of the tools God uses to help guide us to maturity. Make no mistake: *Prayer is work.* It's fun to see God's answers, but it's not always fun to pray—especially when perseverance is involved. And yet, as we pray, we can find ourselves—and our perspective—transformed. C. S.

Lewis had it right when he said that prayer doesn't change God; it changes us. Similarly, Oswald Chambers once observed that to say "prayer changes things" is not as close to the truth as saying "prayer changes me and then I change things."

As you pray for your children, then, I'd encourage you to look beyond the work God is doing in their lives and grab hold of the ways he will use your prayers to build and strengthen your own faith. Remember: Prayer represents an opportunity for you to partner with God in accomplishing his purposes here on earth. God *wants* you to pray—Scripture makes that perfectly clear—but how, when, and even whether you choose to take advantage of the opportunity he offers is entirely up to you.

Using the Bible as the basis for your prayers—as we have in this book—is just one of many methods you can utilize in praying for your children. I believe that God also speaks to us today through the Holy Spirit, prompting us to pray by means of a sensation that is vaguely similar to the familiar "mother's intuition." When you sense God leading you to pray for your kids or for a specific situation they are involved in, go for it— with or without a Bible verse in hand.

Another valuable prayer tool is to keep a journal. Few exercises are as faith-building and perspective-changing as reading back through your prayers and discovering how God has answered them. When the going gets tough—when you find yourself in the faith-stretching position of having to pray with perseverance—put yourself in the place of the fellow who wrote Psalm 77. Troubled and in great distress, he cried out to the Lord again and again—and found himself wondering whether God's promises had failed. But then he stopped to consider what God had done. "I will remember your miracles of long ago," he said. "I will meditate on all your works and consider all your mighty deeds."[1] This simple act of reflection—of remembering and dwelling on the things God had already done—was enough to catapult the psalmist from questions to confidence, from anxiety to assurance, and from discouragement to praise. Likewise, when you stop to reconsider the ways God has already answered your prayers and the wondrous things he has done in your children's lives, it becomes much easier to have faith for the future—and to keep pressing on in prayer.

Finally, do not underestimate the power of "multiplied prayer." Jesus promises that "if two of you on earth agree about anything you ask for, it will be done for you by my Father in heaven."[2] Joining or starting a Moms In Touch group is a great way to access the power of multiplied prayer. Another option is to copy my friend Annesley's idea: Each month, she solicited information from ten or twelve of our college friends, and then sent each of us a newsletter composed almost entirely of prayer requests for our children. In addition to being an innovative prayer tool, Annesley's prayer updates provided a welcome way for far-flung friends to stay in touch.

All it takes to tap into Christ's "two or more" promise is one other person. If you have been praying alone, ask God to give you a prayer partner, preferably someone who knows your kids and who can understand their needs. Years ago, when our children were quite young, God prompted me to ask my friend Margaret to join me in prayer. You can imagine my delight when I learned that God had put my name on her heart at the very same time! We began meeting together for an hour or so each week. Now, even though we are separated by three thousand miles, we still pray for each other's families; when one of my kids has a specific need, all I need to do is pick up the phone or send an e-mail message, and I know Margaret will join me in prayer, bringing the promise of Matthew 18:20 to fulfillment.

Praying the Scriptures for your children, following the prayer promptings of the Holy Spirit, keeping a prayer journal, and joining your prayers with the prayers of others are just a few of the many ways you can respond to God's invitation—his command—to pray.

No doubt you will find and use other methods. As you enter the proving ground, my prayer for you is from Hebrews 12:1–2, namely, that you will run with perseverance the race marked out for you, fixing your eyes on Jesus, the author and perfecter of your faith. As you keep your gaze focused on him, you will discover that no matter how many gifts or blessings he showers on your children, God alone is the ultimate answer to all of your prayers. You will find that he is, as he assured Abraham in Genesis 15:1, "your shield, your very great reward."

USING BIBLICAL
CHARACTERS TO PRAY
FOR YOUR CHILDREN

PRAYING THE SCRIPTURES FOR YOUR CHILDREN BY INSERTING THEIR names into specific verses is just one way you can use the Bible to energize your prayer life. Another powerful prayer strategy is to use the example of biblical characters—real human beings with real strengths and weaknesses—as an inspiration for your prayers.

Take Peter, for instance. I have always felt a kinship with Peter. Bold and brash, he's the one who blathered on and on about putting up shelters for Moses and Elijah when they appeared with Jesus on the top of the mountain, making plans and talking incessantly until he was finally interrupted by God Almighty—and suddenly found himself facedown on the ground, terrified. He's the one who jumped in to "save" Jesus, cutting off the ear of one of the high priest's servants before Jesus put a stop to his ill-considered zeal. And he's the one who, when the going got tough, denied—three times—that he ever knew Jesus.

Who couldn't relate to a guy like that? And yet, despite his human failings, God used Peter mightily. *What*, I wondered, *made Peter so . . . well, so useable?*

I was reading the book of Acts the other day, giving no real thought to Peter, when suddenly there he was. As I read about him (in Acts 2–4), I couldn't help but be amazed by all of his positive attributes. For example, Peter obviously knew the Scriptures backwards and forwards, and he used them to interpret what was happening in the days following Jesus' death and resurrection. As he talked to an audience of fellow Jews—some of the very folks who had demanded Jesus' death—he didn't scorn or condemn them; rather, he offered hope and encouragement, both for them and for future generations. He used the occasion of an incredible miracle—the healing of a crippled man—not to draw attention to himself but to point the way to Jesus. And, when the big guns showed up and tried to put a muzzle on him, Peter refused to cave in under the pressure. Instead, Acts 4 tells us, he was filled with the Holy Spirit, demonstrated remarkable courage, and proved that he feared and obeyed God rather than humans—even when it meant he had to go to prison.

> *Lord, make my children like Peter. They are human and they are weak, but make them useable. Give them a ready knowledge of the Bible, let them offer the hope of the gospel to a hurting world, and let them always seek to point the*

way to you rather than try to gain glory for themselves. Fill them with your Holy Spirit, give them the courage to stand firm in the face of peer pressure and negative influences, and cause them to love you, to fear you, and to obey you more than they love, fear, or obey any human being.

What a great prayer! I didn't make it up—it came straight out of a couple of chapters in the Bible. I wasn't even looking for a prayer when I was reading Acts, but once I spotted Peter, I couldn't pass up the opportunity to turn his life into a prayer for my family. The Bible is full—bursting, actually—with similar prayer opportunities. Even folks like Enoch—who pops up briefly in Genesis 5 (verses 21–24) and gets only the bare minimum of subsequent biblical press coverage—can spark our prayers:

Lord, let Robbie be like Enoch. Let him walk with you.

As you read your Bible, be alert to the people you meet. Who are they? What makes them tick? What character traits or attributes do they possess that enable them to do God's work? What weaknesses have they had to overcome? Ask God to open your eyes to the prayer possibilities afforded by these men and women who have left their mark on history.

Another—more direct—approach to using biblical characters as the basis for your prayers is to simply pick a character to study, and then use his or her attributes as a springboard for your prayers. I've listed several familiar folks below, along with a handful of their distinguishing characteristics. Choose one of these people, or select someone else whose traits mirror those you would like God to develop in your children.

Like Peter, these people are flawed. They have all made mistakes. They are all sinners—just like all of us. But by focusing on their strengths instead of on their weaknesses, we can prayerfully "borrow" their godly attributes as we ask God to shape and use our kids for his kingdom.

Abraham: The Father of Nations

- A powerful, confident pray-er (see Genesis 18:23–33)
- Obedient to God (see Genesis 12:4; 22:3)
- Unselfish, generous (see Genesis 13:8–9)
- A tither, acknowledged God's provision (see Genesis 14:20)
- Faithful, trusted God (see Genesis 22:3–12; Hebrews 11:17)

Ruth: The Faithful Daughter

- Loving daughter-in-law, valued family ties (see Ruth 1:16–17)
- Hard worker, industrious (see Ruth 2:7, 23)
- Obedient, honored her mother-in-law (see Ruth 3:5)
- Patient (see Ruth 3:18)
- Well-known for her noble character (see Ruth 3:11)

David: Israel's Greatest King

- Courageous (see 1 Samuel 17:34–36)
- Refused to listen to fear, discouragement, or negative people (see 1 Samuel 17:28–37)
- Zealous for God, knew the power of God's name (see 1 Samuel 17:45–46)
- Contrite spirit, repentant after sin (see Psalm 51)
- A man after God's own heart (see 1 Samuel 13:14)

Elizabeth: The Patient Mother

- Patient, waited on God's timing for a son, gave God credit for the blessing instead of blame for the delay (see Luke 1:25)

- Used by God to bless and encourage Mary (see Luke 1:42)
- Righteous, humble, took God's word seriously (see Luke 1:6, 43)
- Full of faith (see Luke 1:45)
- Hospitable (see Luke 1:56)

Gideon: The Mighty Warrior

- Humble (see Judges 6:15)
- Worshipful (see Judges 6:24; 7:15)
- Obedient to God (see Judges 6:27; 7:1–8)
- Tactful, diplomatic (see Judges 8:1–3)
- Deflected glory from himself, pointed others toward God (Judges 8:22–23)

Rebekah: Isaac's Pure Bride

- Industrious, hardworking, strong (see Genesis 24:19–20)
- Kind, considerate, respectful toward elders (see Genesis 24:18–19)
- Demonstrated sincere and ready hospitality (see Genesis 24:25)
- A beautiful virgin, sexually pure, modest (see Genesis 24:16, 65)
- Had her family's respect and blessing (see Genesis 24:57–60)

Timothy: An Example to the Believers

- Knew the Scriptures, which equipped him for every good work (see 2 Timothy 3:14–17)
- Had an unbelieving father, followed the teaching of his Christian mother and grandmother (see Acts 16:1; 2 Timothy 1:5)
- Served as an example to others, even in his youth (1 Timothy 4:12)
- Diligent, persevering, collaborated with Paul to preach the gospel (1 Timothy 4:15–16; 1 Corinthians 16:10–11)

- An adept problem solver, pointed people to Jesus (see 1 Corinthians 4:17)

Esther: The Beautiful Queen

- Obedient and respectful toward her father/cousin (see Esther 2:20)
- Loyal to her people, patriotic (see Esther 8:3–6)
- Courageous, heroic, self-sacrificing (see Esther 4:11–16; 7:6)
- Beautiful in appearance and spirit, favored by all (see Esther 2:15–17)
- A compassionate intercessor (see Esther 4:4–5; 8:3–6)

Joseph: The Visionary Manager

- A gifted administrator, manager, organizer, planner (see Genesis 39:4–6, 22–23; 41:41, 49, 56–57)
- Sexually pure, resisted temptation (see Genesis 39:7–13)
- Depended on God, acknowledged his sovereignty (see Genesis 41:16; 45:8)
- Loved and honored his father (see Genesis 45:23; 47:7; 50:1–3)
- Forgiving, overcame hurt and rejection (see Genesis 50:16–21)

Daniel: The Statesman-Prophet

- Smart and handsome, yet humble (see Daniel 1:4; 9:18; 10:12, 17)
- Self-controlled, trustworthy, and pure (see Daniel 1:8; 6:4; 10:3)
- Wise in all things, including his choice of friends (see Daniel 1:17–20; 2:17)
- Prayerful, trusted God (Daniel 2:18; 6:10, 23)
- Feared God and not men, courageous, didn't hide his faith (see Daniel 5:22–23; 6:10)

RECOMMENDED READING AND OTHER RESOURCES

I AM GRATEFUL TO THE FOLLOWING AUTHORS FOR THE WAYS IN which their books have helped shape my attitudes on prayer and parenting. While there are many excellent resources available to today's parents, I recommend these in the hope that they will encourage, challenge, and inspire you as much as they have me.

Blue, Ron and Judy. *Raising Money-Smart Kids*. Nashville: Nelson, 1992.

A practical, biblically based guidebook for teaching kids (and parents, too!) the secrets of earning, saving, investing, and spending money wisely.

Fleming, Jean. *A Mother's Heart: A Look at Values, Vision, and Character for the Christian Mother*. Colorado Springs: NavPress, 1996.

A "must-read" for Christian moms who want to develop the values, vision, and character we need in order to be thankful for our children and to thoroughly enjoy being a mother.

Fuller, Cheri. *When Mothers Pray*. Sisters, Ore.: Multnomah, 1997.

Offers encouragement, motivation, and creative tips and strategies for moms who want to influence their children's lives through the power of prayer.

Heald, Cynthia. *Becoming a Woman of Prayer*. Colorado Springs: NavPress, 1996.

Encourages us to grow in our intimacy with God by explaining what the Bible teaches about prayer. Makes a great Bible study for individuals or small groups.

Omartian, Stormie. *The Power of a Praying Parent*. Eugene, Ore.: Harvest House, 1995.

Offers thirty short, easy-to-read chapters designed to help moms pray through every age and stage of a child's life. Makes a valuable daily devotional tool.

Sheets, Dutch. *Intercessory Prayer: Discover How God Can Use Your Prayers to Move Heaven and Earth*. Ventura, Calif.: Regal, 1997.

The most inspiring, interesting, insightful, and informative book on prayer I have ever read. It will revolutionize your prayer life!

Yates, John & Susan. *What Really Matters at Home: Eight Crucial Elements for Building Character in Your Family*. Dallas: Word, 1992.

A biblical, practical, fun book for those who want to build character—from integrity and faith to compassion and courage—in their family.

Also, if you are not already involved in a Moms In Touch group, consider joining one (or starting one!). I know of no better way to energize your prayer life and effectively cover your children, their teachers, and their school in prayer. To find out about Moms In Touch in your area, to obtain information on starting a group, or simply to learn more about the four steps of prayer that make the Moms In Touch hour of prayer so powerful, contact:

Moms In Touch International
P.O. Box 1120
Poway, California 92074-1120
(858) 486-4065
E-mail address: info@MomsInTouch.org
Web site: www.MomsInTouch.org

Notes

Introduction: Getting Started in Prayer

1. John Wesley and Andrew Murray, as quoted by Dutch Sheets in *Intercessory Prayer: How God Can Use Your Prayers to Move Heaven and Earth* (Ventura, Calif.: Regal, 1997), 23, 30.

2. See Psalm 2:8; 2 Chronicles 7:14; Matthew 7:7 (italics added).

3. Hebrews 4:12 AMPLIFIED

4. Jack Hayford, *Prayer Is Invading the Impossible* (South Plainfield, N.J.: Logos International, 1977), 92.

Chapter One: Praying for Your Child's Salvation

1. Observed by Henry T. Blackaby in *Experiencing God* (Nashville: Lifeway, 1990), 64.

2. Jeanne Hendricks, *A Mother's Legacy* (Colorado Springs: NavPress, 1992), 99.

3. You can read Elizabeth's story in Luke 1.

4. Hebrews 10:36

Chapter Three: Praying for Your Child's Gifts

1. John & Susan Yates, *What Really Matters at Home: Eight Crucial Elements for Building Character in Your Family* (Dallas: Word, 1992), 134.

2. See Jeremiah 1:5.

3. See Acts 1:4–8.

Chapter Four: Praying for Your Child to Promote God's Kingdom

1. Susan Martins Miller, *Hudson Taylor* (Uhrichsville, Ohio: Barbour, 1993), 64.

2. Quoted in Mrs. Howard Taylor, *Behind the Ranges* (Greenwood, S.C.: Lutterworth, 1959), 25.

Chapter Five: Praying for Wisdom and Discernment
1. You can read this story in 1 Kings 3:5–14.
2. Quoted in Cynthia Heald, *Becoming a Woman of Prayer* (Colorado Springs: NavPress, 1996), 69.
3. Colossians 1:9 THE MESSAGE
4. Colossians 2:3
5. Eugene Peterson, *The Message: The New Testament, Psalms and Proverbs in Contemporary Language* (Colorado Springs: NavPress, 1995), 862.

Chapter Six: Praying for a Servant's Heart
1. Matthew 20:26–28
2. Bill Gothard, *Advanced Seminar Textbook* (Oak Brook, Ill.: Institute in Basic Life Principles, 1986), 358.
3. You can read this story in 1 Samuel 18–20.
4. See 1 Samuel 18:1.

Chapter Seven: Praying for Kindness and Compassion
1. John & Susan Yates, *What Really Matters at Home: Eight Crucial Elements for Building Character in Your Family* (Dallas: Word, 1992), 70.
2. See Luke 10:25–37.
3. Lamentations 3:22

Chapter Eight: Praying for Self-Control, Diligence, and Self-Discipline
1. See Proverbs 25:28; 13:3–4; 5:22–23.

Chapter Nine: Praying for Physical Health and Safety
1. See Isaiah 49:16.
2. 2 Samuel 12:23
3. Bonnie Shepherd, "When Moms Pray," *Focus on the Family* magazine, vol. 23, no. 8 (August 1999), 4.

4. *Heart to Heart,* vol. 11, no. 2, Fall 1999 (Moms In Touch International).

5. Jeremiah 33:3

Chapter Ten: Praying for Spiritual Protection

1. C. S. Lewis, *The Screwtape Letters* (New York: Macmillan, 1982), 3.

2. See 2 Corinthians 11:14–15.

3. See 2 Corinthians 12:9.

4. You can read this story in 1 Samuel 1–3.

5. 1 Samuel 2:21

Chapter Eleven: Praying for Your Child's Emotional Well-Being

1. See Romans 14:7–9; Genesis 1:27.

2. See Psalm 139:14; Romans 5:8; 8:38–39.

3. See Matthew 5:7; 18:21–22.

4. See Luke 6:27–28.

5. Luke 6:31

6. Warren Wiersbe, *Be Joyful* (Colorado Springs: Chariot Victor, 1974).

7. Psalm 90:14, emphasis added

Chapter Twelve: Praying for Kids in Crisis

1. 2 Kings 4:22

2. 2 Kings 4:30

3. Noted in Henry T. Blackaby & Claude V. King, *Experiencing God* (Nashville: Lifeway, 1990), 108.

4. Jim Cymbala with Dean Merrill, *Fresh Wind, Fresh Fire* (Grand Rapids: Zondervan, 1997), 60–62.

5. Cymbala, *Fresh Wind, Fresh Fire,* 56.

6. See Cymbala, *Fresh Wind, Fresh Fire,* 19.

7. Research cited in Young Life's *Relationships* magazine (Fall/Winter 1998), 9.

8. James Dobson, *Emotions: Can You Trust Them?* (Ventura, Calif.: Regal, 1980), 133.

Chapter Thirteen: Praying for Your Child's Relationship . . . with Friends

1. Chuck Swindoll, *Insight for Living* radio broadcast (23 August 1999).

Chapter Fourteen: Praying for Your Child's Relationship . . . with Siblings

1. You can read the story in Genesis 25 and 27.
2. You can read the story in Genesis 32–33.
3. Genesis 32:11–12
4. You can read the story in Genesis 4.

Chapter Fifteen: Praying for Your Child's Relationship . . . with Teachers and Coaches

1. Matthew 9:37

Chapter Sixteen: Praying for Your Child's Relationship . . . with You

1. James Dobson, *Dare to Discipline* (Wheaton, Ill.: Tyndale House, 1992), 18.
2. Exodus 20:12

Chapter Seventeen: Praying for Your Child's Purpose in Life

1. Esther 4:14
2. See Isaiah 43:1; Jeremiah 1:5.
3. Psalm 139:13, 16
4. Noted in Jean Fleming, *A Mother's Heart: A Look at Values, Vision, and Character for the Christian Mother* (Colorado Springs: NavPress, 1996), 89.
5. See Romans 8:28.
6. See Luke 1.

Chapter Eighteen: Praying for Your Child's Marriage

1. Genesis 24:12–14
2. Nathaniel and Andrew Ryun, *It's a Lifestyle: Discipleship in Our Relationships* (Lawrence, Kans.: Silver Clarion Press, 1996), 67.

Chapter Nineteen: Praying for Your Child's Management of Time and Money

1. You can read the story in Luke 21:1–4.

Chapter Twenty: Praying for Your Child When He or She Leaves Your Nest

1. You can read Jennifer's story in my book, *Celebration of Miracles* (Nashville: Nelson, 1995).
2. See Exodus 3:11–12
3. David Wilkerson, "The Power of the Lord's Presence," *Times Square Church Pulpit Series* (7 December 1998).
4. Joshua 1:9
5. See Genesis 8:20; 28:18–19; Exodus 17:15.
6. Philippians 4:6 LB

Conclusion: The Life-Changing Work of Prayer

1. Psalm 77:11–12
2. Matthew 18:19

We want to hear from you. Please send your comments about this book to us in care of the address below. Thank you.

ZondervanPublishingHouse
Grand Rapids, Michigan 49530
http://www.zondervan.com